IN RECITAL®
WITH POPULAR MUSIC

ABOUT THE SERIES • A NOTE TO THE TEACHER

In Recital® with Popular Music is a wonderful collection of popular arrangements. Disney favorites, current popular favorites, show tunes, and old-time classics make this series a delightful mix of popular music for everyone! The two outstanding arrangers of this series, Edwin McLean and Kevin Olson, have created engaging arrangements of some of the best popular pieces, all of which have been carefully leveled to ensure success with this repertoire. We know that to motivate, the teacher must challenge the student with attainable goals. This series makes that possible. You will find favorites that are easy to sing along with as well as recital-style arrangements. This series complements other FJH publications and will help you plan student recital repertoire. The books include CDs with complete performances designed to assist with recital preparation. Throughout this series you will find interesting background information for each piece by Dave and Becky Olsen.

Use the enclosed CD as a teaching and motivational tool. For a guide to listening to the CD, turn to page 43.

Production: Frank J. Hackinson
Production Coordinators: Joyce Loke and Satish Bhakta
Cover Art Concept: Helen Marlais
Cover Design: Terpstra Design, San Francisco, CA
Cover Illustration: Sophie Library
Engraving: Tempo Music Press, Inc.
Printer: Tempo Music Press, Inc.

ISBN 1-56939-751-1

ORGANIZATION OF THE SERIES
IN RECITAL® WITH POPULAR MUSIC

The series is carefully leveled into the following six categories: Early Elementary, Elementary, Late Elementary, Early Intermediate, Intermediate, and Late Intermediate. Each of the works has been selected for its artistic as well as its pedagogical merit.

Book Three — Late Elementary, reinforces the following concepts:

- Eighth notes, dotted quarter notes, and triplets are added to the basic notes students played in books 1 and 2. Syncopation is used.

- Students play different articulations such as *legato* and *staccato* at the same time.

- Melodies are played in the left as well as the right hand.

- Students play pieces in a variety of different moods and tempos.

- Pieces reinforce five-finger scales, as well as scale patterns that extend from the usual five-finger patterns (with finger crossings).

- Blocked intervals up to a sixth, double thirds, and use of the pedal to create a big sound as well as to play artistically.

- Keys of C major, G major, F major, D major, and A minor.

The Best of Both Worlds and *Ja-Da* were arranged as optional duets. However, these pieces can be played as solos as well. *The Chicken Dance* was arranged as an equal-part duet.

TABLE OF CONTENTS

About the Pieces and Composers

Chim Chim Cher-ee

Chim Chim Cher-ee is the Academy Award winning song from the 1964 Disney classic film *Mary Poppins*. Written and composed by Richard and Robert Sherman, the song helped the Sherman Brothers collect both an Oscar and a Grammy award. Their inspiration for the song came from one of the movie's screenwriters, Don DeGradi, who explained to them that British folklore promoted the belief that shaking hands with a chimney sweep would bring good luck. *"Good luck will rub off, when I shakes 'ands with you."*

All I Have to Do Is Dream

All I Have to Do Is Dream was written and composed by the legendary Boudleaux Bryant, and was a milestone hit record for the Everly Brothers, Don and Phil, back in 1958. This song has the distinction of being the only song to hold the No. 1 position on all of Billboard magazine's singles charts during a particular week—June 2, 1958. Rolling Stone magazine included this song at No. 141 in their *500 Greatest Songs of All-Time* list.

The Best of Both Worlds

For all you *Hannah Montana* fans, here's an arrangement of the theme song from the Disney Channel's most popular show. If you're a fan of the show, then you know that teenager Miley Cyrus created the Hannah persona so she could lead a normal life by day and turn into the pop sensation when necessary. However, at her live concerts, Miley performs the song as herself with Hannah also on stage thanks to the application of IBM's green-screen technology. *"Rock out the show."*

ABOUT THE PIECES AND COMPOSERS

Ja-Da

Written in 1918 by pianist Bob Carleton (his surname often misspelled as Carlton), this song has been a favorite of Dixieland Jazz Bands and jazz musicians for many years. It is one of those rare songs that is appreciated both by instrumentalists and singers. Great singers like Frank Sinatra, Peggy Lee, and Al Jarreau have "covered" (recorded) the song; as have instrumental greats such as trumpeters Al Hirt and Louis Armstrong, tenor saxophonist Sonny Rollins, and pianist Oscar Peterson. *Ja Da, Ja Da, Jing, Jing, Jing!*

Yellow Bird

For this calypso-styled song, the noted choral composer and conductor, Norman Luboff, adapted a Haitian folk song, sometimes called *Ti Zwazo (Little Birds)*, and husband and wife writing team, Alan and Marilyn Bergman, provided the English lyric. The Norman Luboff Choir first recorded the piece in 1957, and a number of other artists of the day quickly covered it. The song continues to be associated with calypso and the Caribbean, and is a favorite for steel drum bands.

She Loves You

Written by John Lennon and Paul McCartney in a hotel room while on tour with rock 'n' roll legend Roy Orbison, this song was first recorded and released as a single in 1963 and helped to launch the Beatles' career. The song broke countless sales records, and was one of five Beatles' songs that held the top five chart positions in Billboard magazine all at the same time—a record that will likely stand for all time. Beatles' producer, George Martin, tried to get the band to change the major 6th chord that ends the song because it was "too jazzy," but the band said, "No, it's a great hook; we've got to do it." Did they ever!

Chim Chim Cher-ee

from Walt Disney's *Mary Poppins*

Music and Lyrics by Richard M. Sherman
and Robert B. Sherman
arr. Kevin Olson

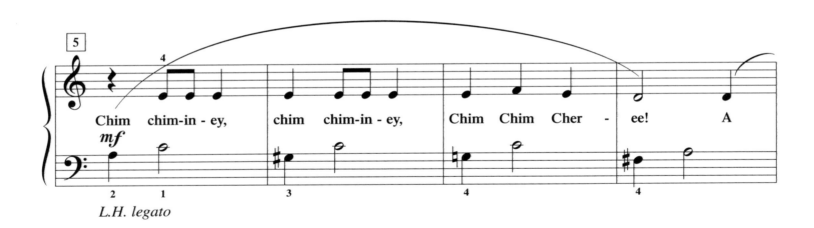

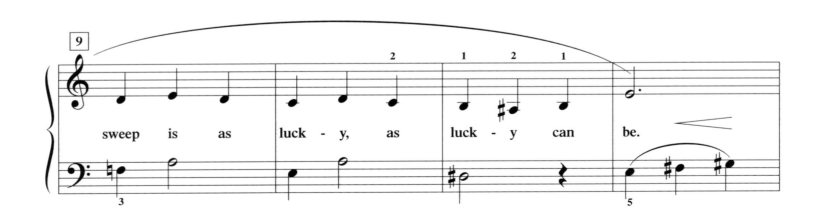

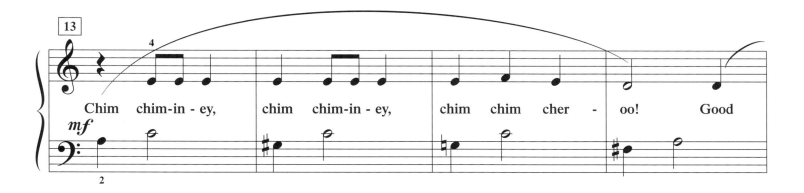

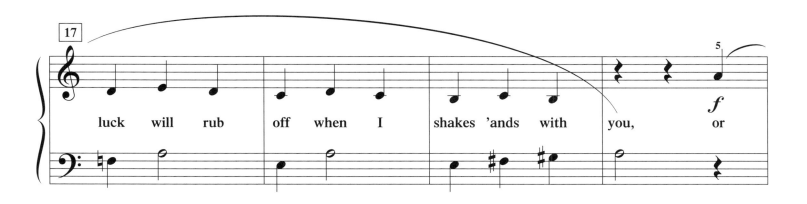

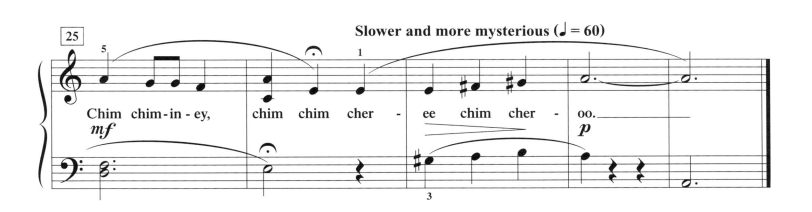

All I Have to Do Is Dream

Music and Lyrics by Boudleaux Bryant
arr. Edwin McLean

When I want you in my arms, when I want you
I feel blue in the night, and I need you

and all your charms,
to hold me tight, } when-ev-er I want you___ all I have to do is

dream,_____ dream, dream, dream. When dream.___

I can make you mine, taste your lips of wine

The Best of Both Worlds

Music and Lyrics by Matthew Gerrard
and Robbie Nevil
arr. Edwin McLean

Moderately fast (♩ = ca. 126)

mf

You get the lim - o out front, hot-test

styles, ev - 'ry shoe, ev - 'ry col - or. Yeah, when you're fa-mous, it can be kind of

Teacher Accompaniment: (*Student plays one octave higher*)

mp

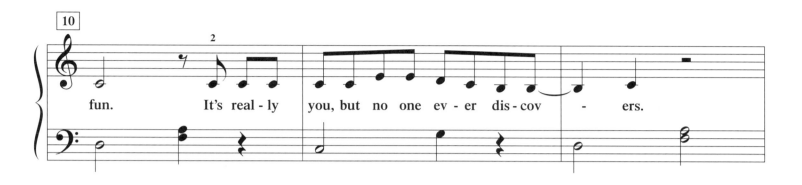

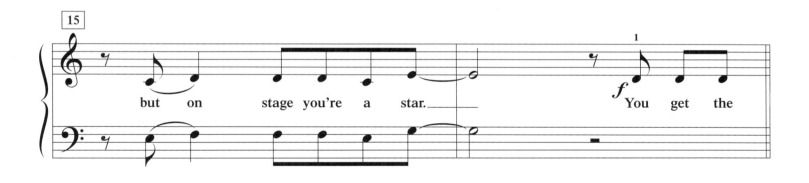

12

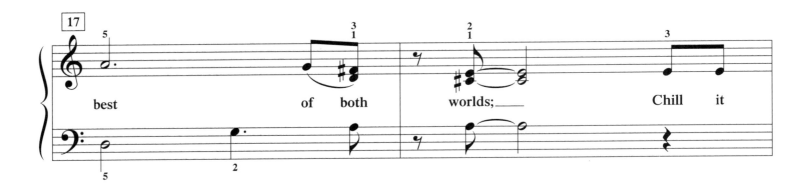

best   of both   worlds;____   Chill   it

out,   take   it   slow,____   then you   rock out the show.____   You   get   the

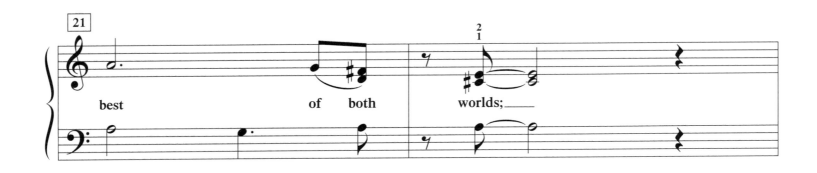

best   of both   worlds;____

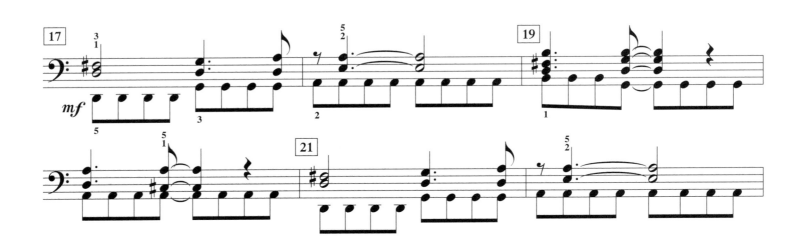

mf

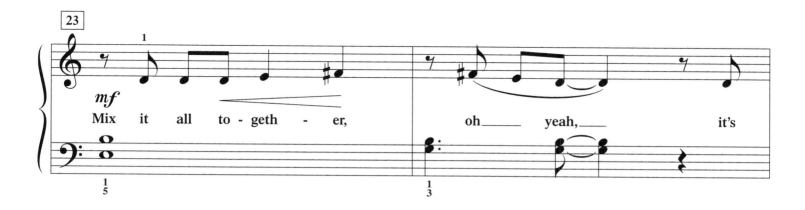

Ja-Da

Music and Lyrics by Bob Carleton
arr. Kevin Olson

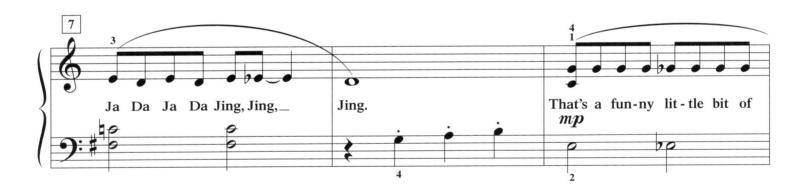

Teacher Accompaniment: *(Student plays one octave higher)*

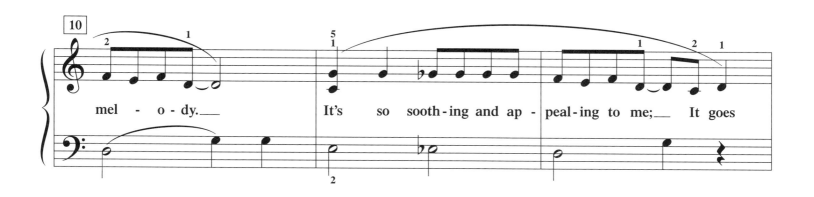

mel - o - dy.___ It's so sooth-ing and ap - peal-ing to me;___ It goes

f Ja Da,___ Ja Da,___ Ja Da Ja Da Jing, Jing,___

p Ja Da Ja Da Jing, Jing,___ *f* Ja Da Ja Da Jing, Jing,___ Jing.

Yellow Bird

Music by Norman Luboff
Lyrics by Charles Alan and Marilyn Bergman
arr. Edwin McLean

With a lazy beat (♩ = ca. 112)

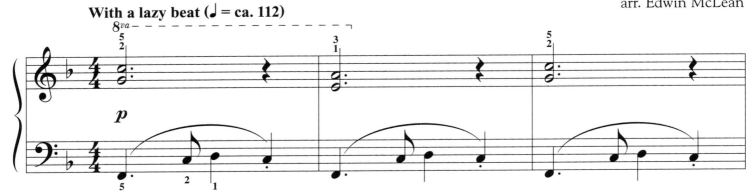

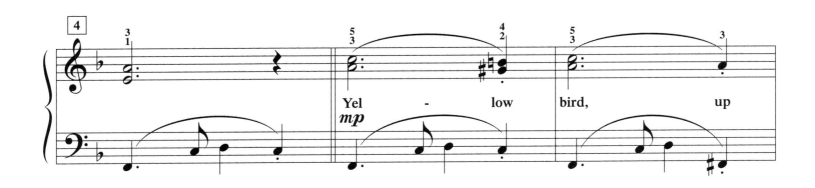

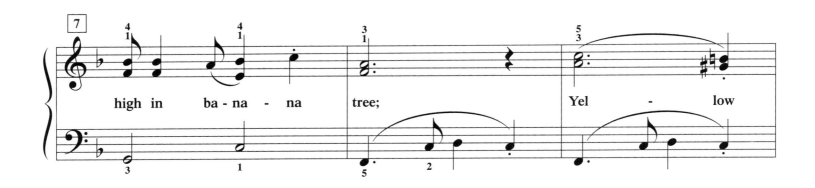

Did your la-dy frien' leave the nest___ a-gain? That is ver - y sad,

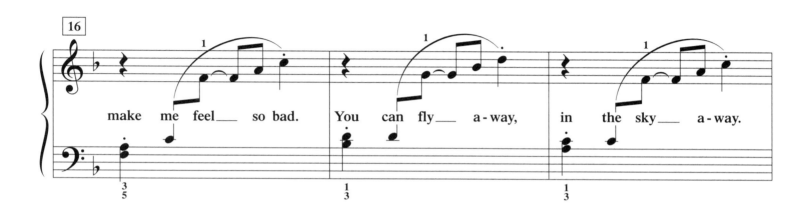

make me feel___ so bad. You can fly___ a-way, in the sky___ a-way.

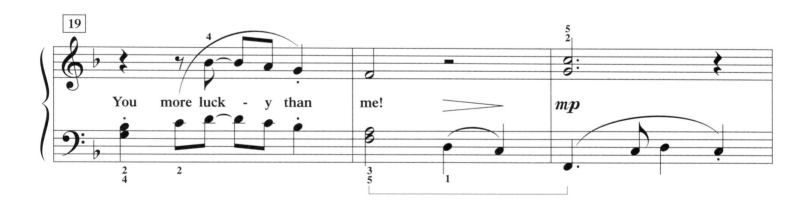

You more luck - y than me!

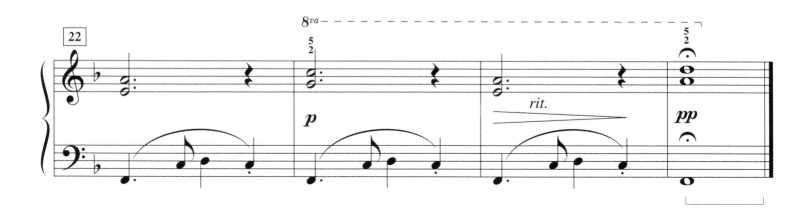

She Loves You

Music and Lyrics by John Lennon
and Paul McCartney
arr. Kevin Olson

With an energetic rock beat (♩ = 144)

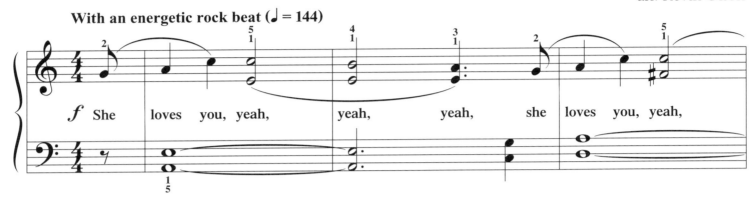

She loves you, yeah, yeah, yeah, she loves you, yeah,

yeah, yeah, she loves you, yeah, yeah, yeah,

yeah! You think you've lost your

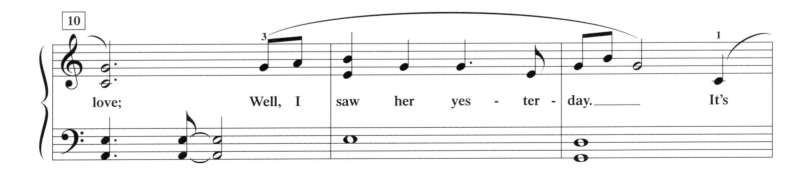

love; Well, I saw her yes - ter - day. It's

you she's think-ing of, and she told me what to

say._____ She says she loves you, and you know that can't be

bad._____ Yes, she loves you, and you

know you should be glad._____ Ooh! She

loves you, yeah, yeah, yeah, she loves you, yeah,

yeah, yeah;___ And with a love like that, you know you should be glad.___

And with a love like that, you

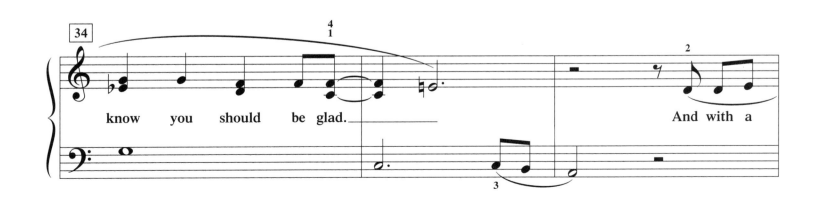

know you should be glad.___ And with a

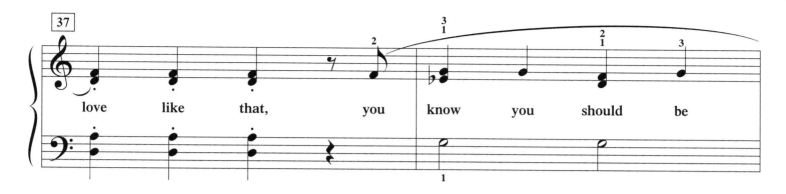

love   like   that,   you   know   you   should   be

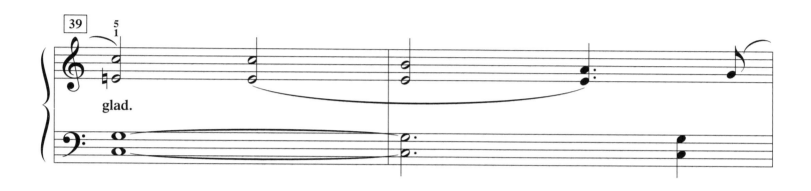

glad.

Yeah,   yeah,   yeah;   Yeah,

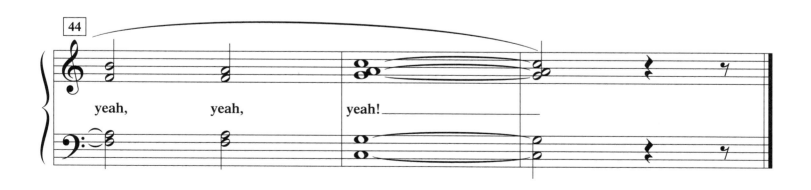

yeah,   yeah,   yeah!

Shine On, Harvest Moon

Music by Nora Bayes-Norworth
Lyrics by Jack Norworth
arr. Edwin McLean

With a steady beat (♩ = ca. 126)

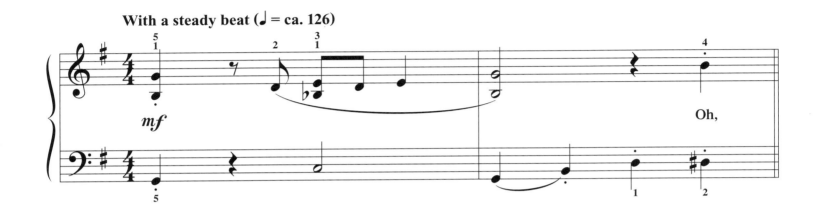

Oh,

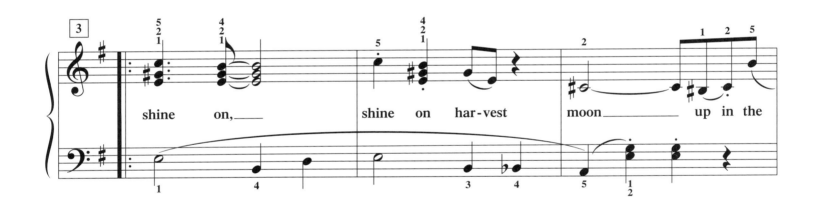

shine on,_____ shine on har-vest moon_____ up in the

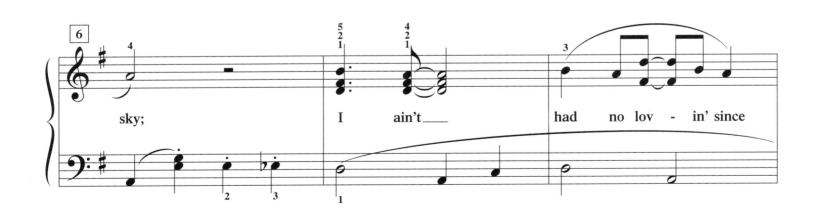

sky; I ain't_____ had no lov - in' since

23

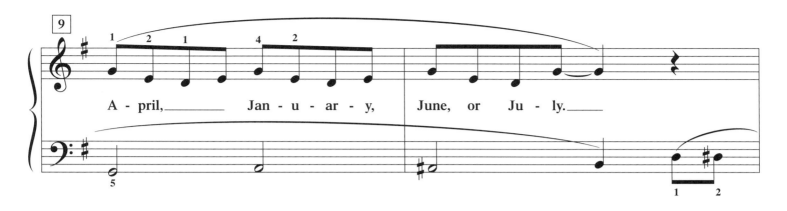

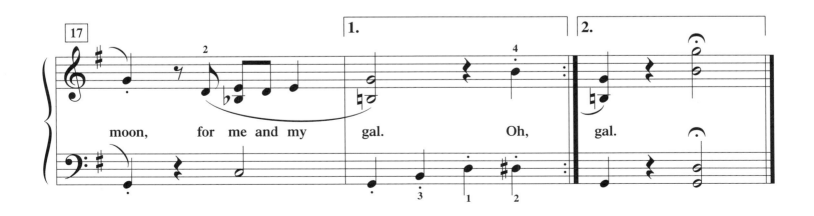

FJH2002

The Chicken Dance
Secondo

Music and Lyrics by Werner Thomas
and Terry Rendall
English Lyrics by Paul Parnes
arr. Kevin Olson

Moderately; in two ($\quad$ = 80)

Play both hands as written

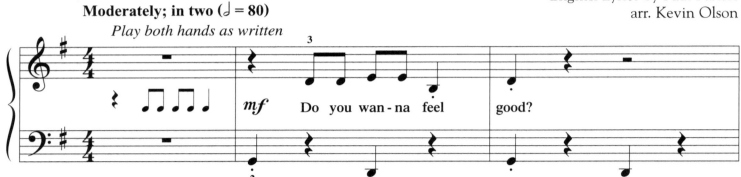

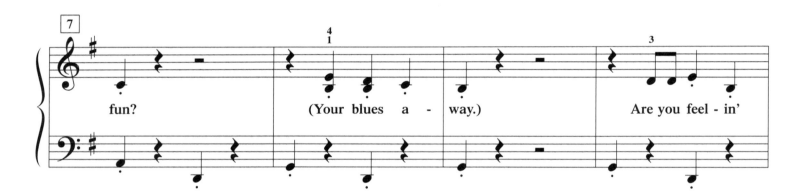

The Chicken Dance
Primo

Music and Lyrics by Werner Thomas
and Terry Rendall
English Lyrics by Paul Parnes
arr. Kevin Olson

Moderately; in two (♩ = 80)
Both hands one octave higher throughout

FJH2002

26

Secondo

Do the Chick-en Dance.

FJH2002

Primo

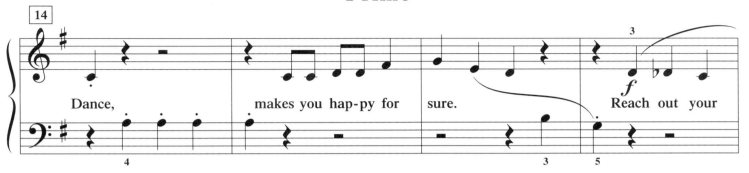

Dance, makes you hap-py for sure. Reach out your

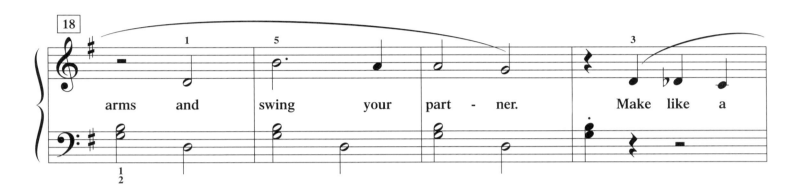

arms and swing your part - ner. Make like a

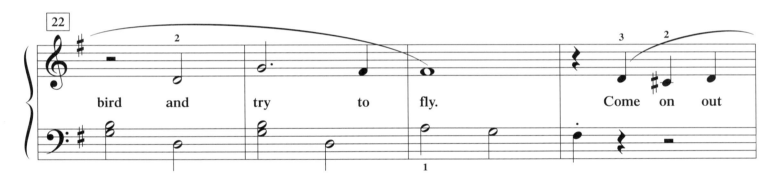

bird and try to fly. Come on out

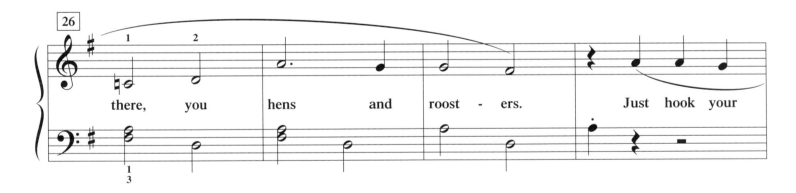

there, you hens and roost - ers. Just hook your

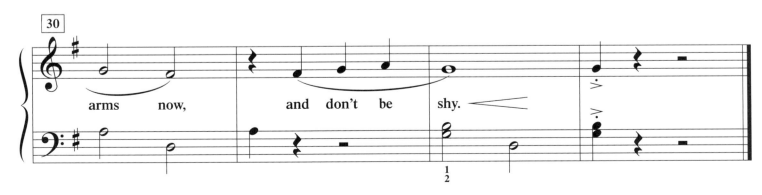

arms now, and don't be shy.

FJH2002

When Irish Eyes Are Smiling

Music by Ernest R. Ball
Lyrics by Chauncey Olcott and George Graff, Jr.
arr. Kevin Olson

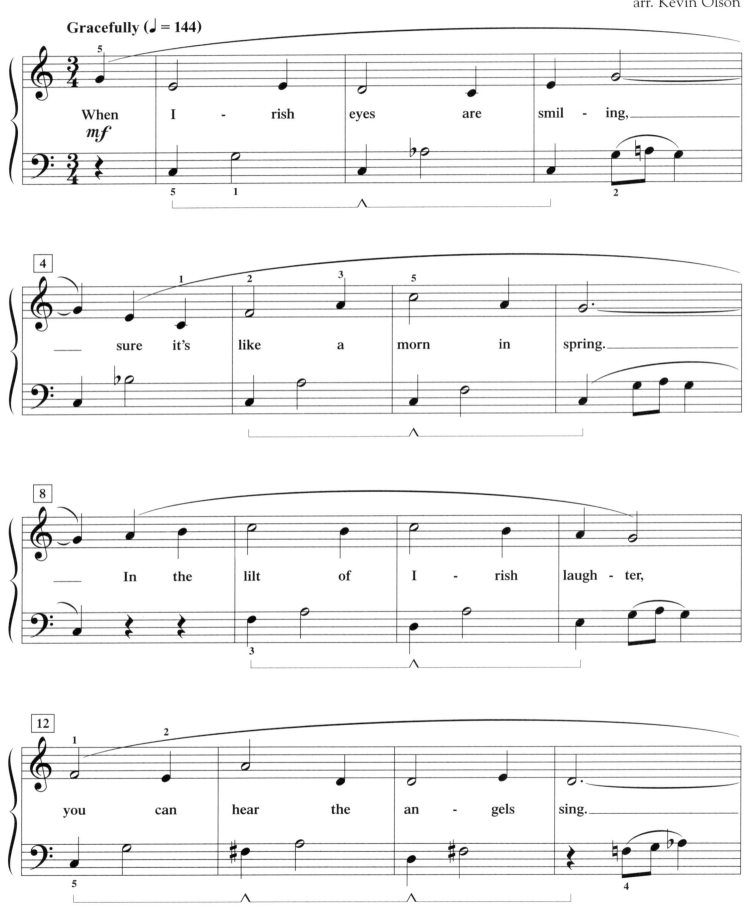

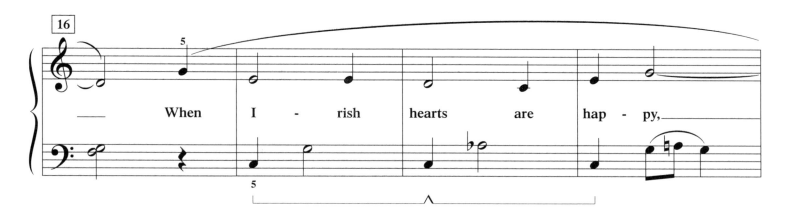

When I - rish hearts are hap - py,

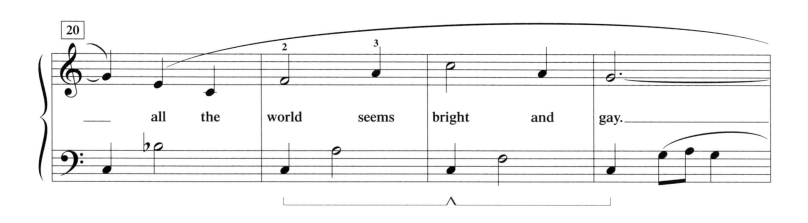

all the world seems bright and gay.

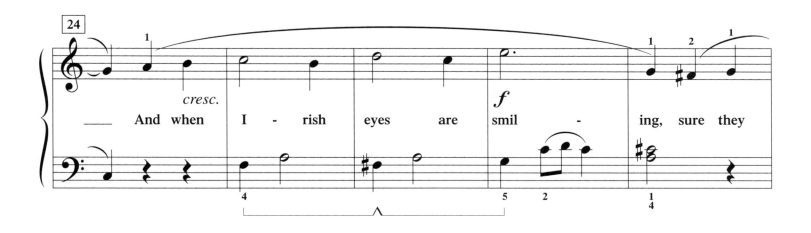

cresc.

And when I - rish eyes are *f* smil - ing, sure they

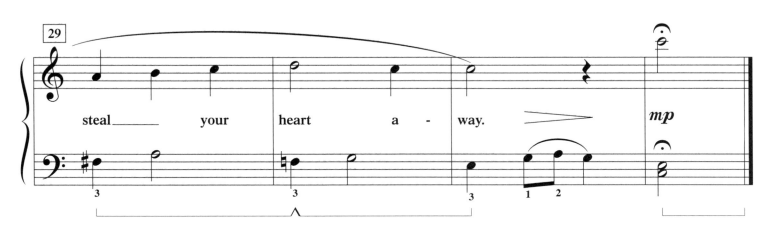

steal_____ your heart a - way. *mp*

The Arkansas Traveler

Southern American Folk Song
arr. Kevin Olson

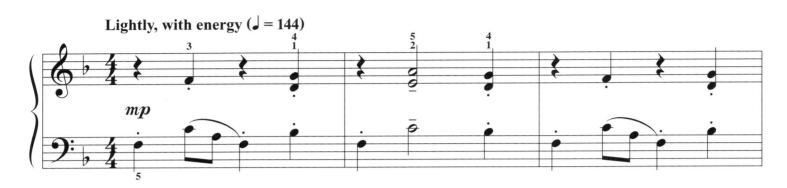

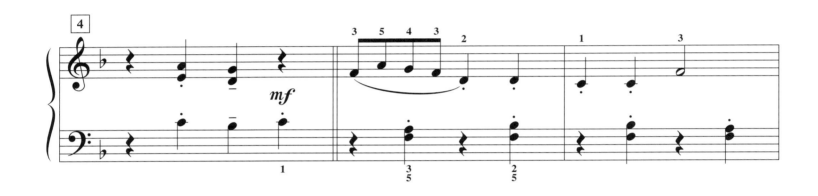

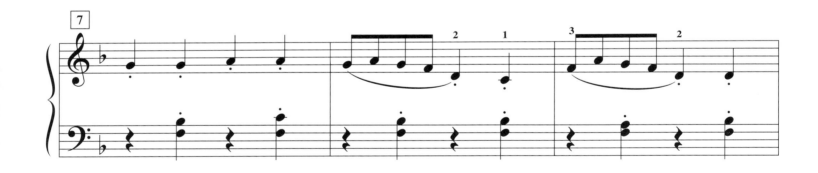

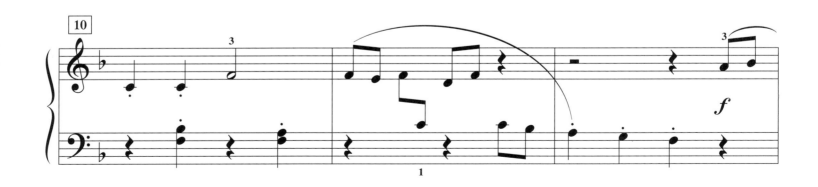

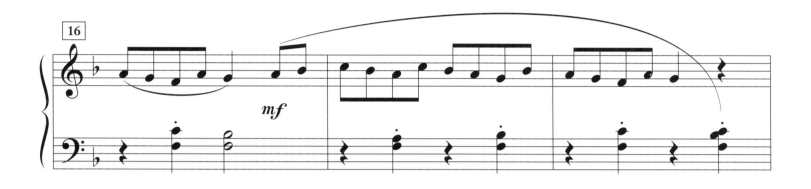

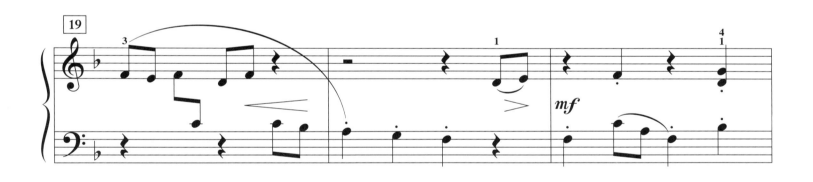

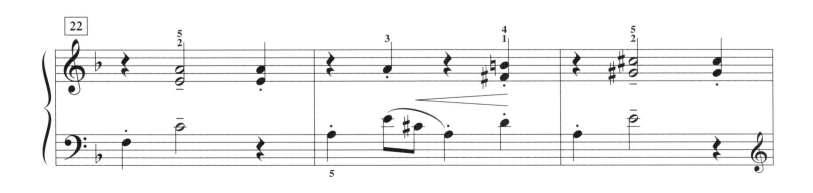

32

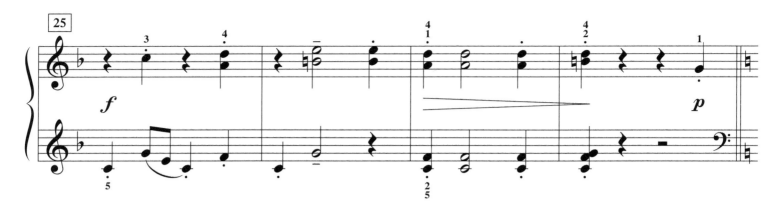

Fly Me to the Moon

(In Other Words)

Music and Lyrics by Bart Howard
arr. Edwin McLean

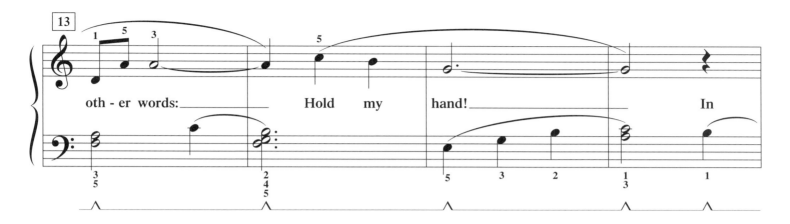

oth - er words:_____ Hold my hand!_____ In

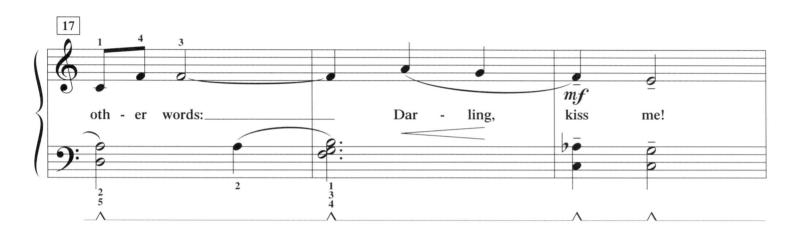

oth - er words:_____ Dar - ling, kiss me!

Fill my heart with song, and let me

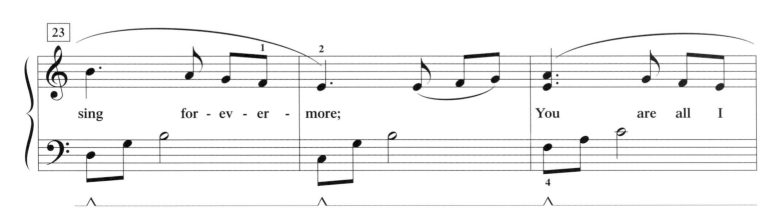

sing for - ev - er - more; You are all I

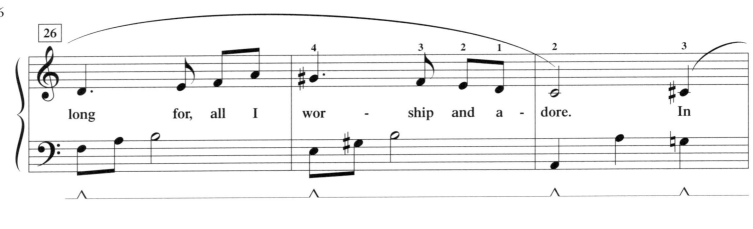

long   for, all   I   wor -   ship and a - dore.   In

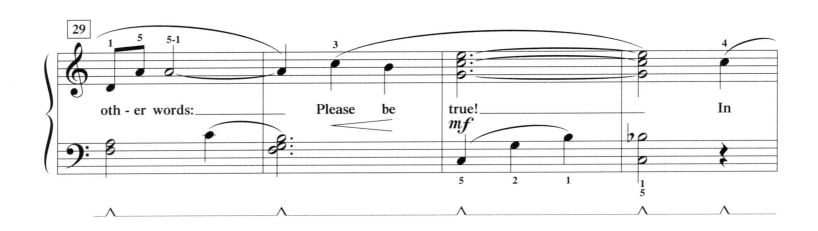

oth - er words: Please   be   true!   In

mf

oth - er words: I   love   you.

mp

R.H.

dim. e rit.

L.H.

L.H.

pp

When I See an Elephant Fly

from Walt Disney's *Dumbo*

Music by Oliver Wallace
Lyrics by Ned Washington

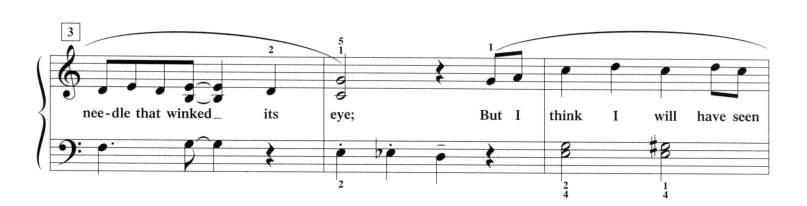

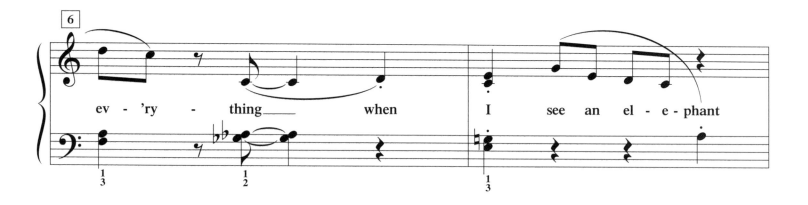

FJH2002

38

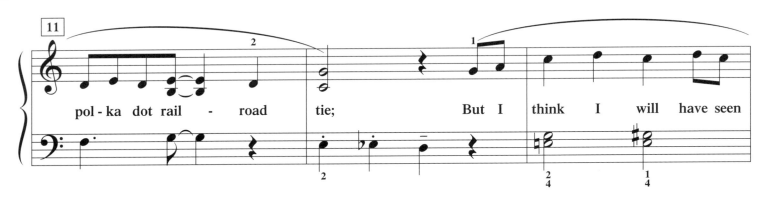

polka dot railroad tie; But I think I will have seen

ev'rything___ when I see an elephant fly.

I saw a clothes-horse rar' up and buck;___ they tell me that a man made a

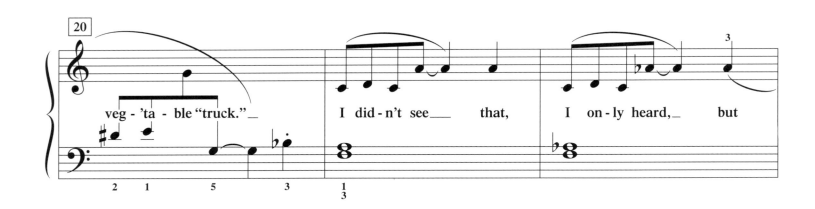

veg'table "truck."___ I didn't see___ that, I only heard,___ but

FJH2002

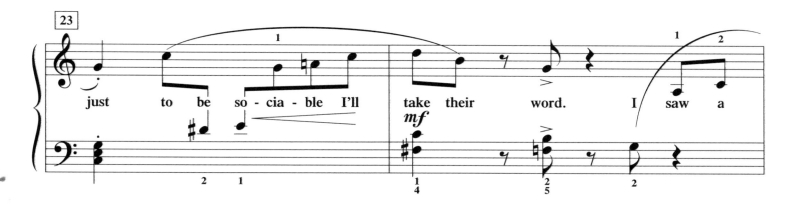

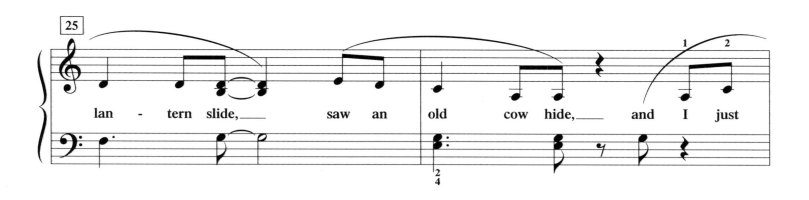

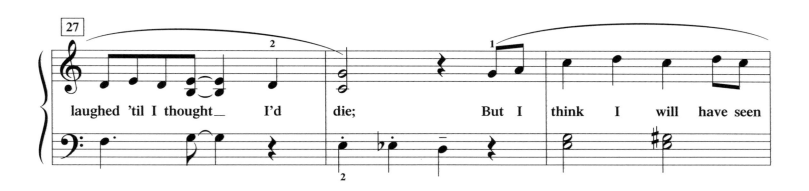

FJH2002

ABOUT THE PIECES AND COMPOSERS

Shine On, Harvest Moon

This classic "Tin Pan Alley" song is credited to the husband and wife team of Nora Bayes and Jack Norworth. Both were popular performers although Nora was much more so, and they premiered this song in the Ziegfeld Follies—a series of elaborate theatrical productions on Broadway—of 1908. The song was an instant success and, to this day, is still being performed and recorded regularly. Nora Bayes' popularity at the time was so great that the legendary songwriter George M. Cohan personally selected her to make the first recording of *Over There*, making it an international success almost overnight. Her image was used on the original sheet music covers for both *Shine On, Harvest Moon* and *Over There*. "Tin Pan Alley" was that part of midtown Manhattan from West 28th Street between Broadway and Sixth Avenue and most of the important music publishers of that era had their offices there.

The Chicken Dance

If you have attended a wedding reception recently, then you might recognize this instrumental dance favorite. Originally entitled *Der Vogerltanz* (The Bird Dance), this oom-pah styled song was written by a Swiss accordion player named Werner Thomas who used to play it in restaurants and hotels. A Belgian record producer heard it, had it recorded, and the rest is history. The song now boasts over 140 recordings having sold in excess of 40 million records.

When Irish Eyes Are Smiling

Here's a favorite about the land of four-leaf clovers and pots o' gold. But the song's composer, Ernest Ball, wasn't from Ireland. He was born in Cleveland, Ohio, and received his classical training at the Cleveland Conservatory. Chauncey Olcott and George Graff, Jr. provided the lyrics, and Olcott actually premiered the song on Broadway in 1912 in a musical entitled *The Isle O' Dreams*—a show which he also produced. Ball and Olcott would go on to write more songs together and work in Vaudeville. Ball was also a charter member of ASCAP (American Society of Composers, Authors, and Publishers) and was inducted into the Songwriters Hall of Fame in 1970. *When Irish Eyes Are Smiling* has been recorded over 200 times and featured in more than twenty film soundtracks.

ABOUT THE PIECES AND COMPOSERS

The Arkansas Traveler

The Arkansas Traveler was written in the mid-1800s by Colonel Sanford C. 'Sandy' Faulkner, who was well-known as a storyteller as well as a fiddler. There are several different lyrics for this piece—the best known written by a government appointed committee so the song could be made the state song of Arkansas in 1949. It lost that distinction in 1963. However, in 1987 it was designated a State Historical Song. If you are a fan of Saturday morning cartoons, you may recognize this piece. Cartoon music maker Carl Stalling used it frequently as background music in the *Merrie Melodies* and *Looney Toons* cartoon series.

Fly Me to the Moon

Fly Me to the Moon is a pop standard written by Bart Howard in 1954. When introduced by Felicia Sanders on the cabaret circuit, it was originally titled *In Other Words*. The song became popularly known as *Fly Me to the Moon* from its first line, but it took a few years for the publishers to change the title officially.

Originally written in $\frac{3}{4}$ waltz-time, Quincy Jones changed it to $\frac{4}{4}$ in his arrangement and gave it a "swing" feel. Accompanied by Count Basie, Frank Sinatra's 1963 recording of this version was a hit, and was played to the astronauts of Apollo 10 on their lunar mission in May 1969.

When I See an Elephant Fly

Here's a clever song from Disney's fourth animated feature *Dumbo*. The movie itself won the 1941 Academy Award for Best Musical Score, but ironically the writers of this song, Oliver Wallace (music) and Ned Washington (lyrics) received a Best Song Oscar, not for this particular song, but instead, *Baby Mine*. Be sure to pay close attention to the chord progression you will play in this song's bridge—the middle part between the two sections of the chorus. It is what jazz musicians call a "Sears and Roebuck" bridge and many jazz players will use this same chord pattern to improvise when they can't remember how the actual bridge of a song is supposed to go.

ABOUT THE ARRANGERS

Edwin McLean

Edwin McLean is a composer living in Chapel Hill, North Carolina. He is a graduate of the Yale School of Music, where he studied with Krzysztof Penderecki and Jacob Druckman. He also holds a master's degrees in music theory and a bachelor's degree in piano performance from the University of Colorado.

Mr. McLean has been the recipient of several grants and awards: The MacDowell Colony, the John Work Award, the Woods Chandler Prize (Yale), Meet the Composer, Florida Arts Council, and many others. He has also won the Aliénor Composition Competition for his work *Sonata for Harpsichord*, published by The FJH Music Company Inc. and recorded by Elaine Funaro (*Into the Millennium*, Gasparo GSCD-331).

Since 1979, Edwin McLean has arranged the music of some of today's best known recording artists. Currently, he is senior editor as well as MIDI orchestrator for The FJH Music Company Inc.

Kevin Olson

Kevin Olson is an active pianist, composer, and faculty member at Elmhurst College near Chicago, Illinois, where he teaches classical and jazz piano, music theory, and electronic music. He holds a Doctor of Education degree from National-Louis University, and bachelor's and master's degrees in music composition and theory from Brigham Young University. Before teaching at Elmhurst College, he held a visiting professor position at Humboldt State University in California.

A native of Utah, Kevin began composing at the age of five. When he was twelve, his composition *An American Trainride* received the Overall First Prize at the 1983 National PTA Convention in Albuquerque, New Mexico. Since then, he has been a composer-in-residence at the National Conference on Piano Pedagogy and has written music for the American Piano Quartet, Chicago a cappella, the Rich Matteson Jazz Festival, and several piano teachers associations around the country.

Kevin maintains a large piano studio, teaching students of a variety of ages and abilities. Many of the needs of his own piano students have inspired a diverse collection of books and solos published by The FJH Music Company Inc., which he joined as a writer in 1994.

USING THE CD

A great way to prepare for your recitals is to listen to the CD.

Enjoy listening to these wonderful pieces anywhere anytime! Listen to them casually (as background music) and attentively. After you have listened to the CD you might discuss interpretation with your teacher and follow along with your score as you listen.

LISTENING ACTIVITY

Listen to the CD and circle the BEST answer:

1. **Circle the piece where you hear eighth-note rhythms played steadily:**

   The Best of Both Worlds (Track 3)

   Ja-Da (Track 4)

2. **Circle the piece that has an introduction:**

   She Loves You (Track 6)

   Yellow Bird (Track 5)

3. **Circle the piece that is gentle and smooth:**

   When Irish Eyes Are Smiling (Track 9)

   Shine On, Harvest Moon (Track 7)

4. **Circle the piece that is cheerful and full of energy:**

   Fly Me to the Moon (Track 11)

   The Chicken Dance (Track 8)

5. **Circle the piece where you hear syncopation:**

   When I See an Elephant Fly (Track 12)

   The Arkansas Traveler (Track 10)

6. **Circle the piece that has an upbeat:**

   Chim Chim Cher-ee (Track 1)

   All I Have to Do Is Dream (Track 2)

Which piece(s) is/are your FAVORITE?

_____

_____

_____

_____

Answers: 1. The Best of Both Worlds 2. Yellow Bird 3. When Irish Eyes Are Smiling 4. The Chicken Dance 5. When I See an Elephant Fly 6. All I Have to Do Is Dream

FJH2002

IN RECITAL®

Helen Marlais

The *In Recital®* series is a fabulous and diverse collection of motivational repertoire for the early elementary to late intermediate pianist. The fine composers/arrangers of this series have created engaging original solos, duets, and arrangements of famous classical themes, jazz works, and Christmas music. This variety of genres also includes selections written for holidays throughout the year. All books include CDs with complete performances. Performance strategies and rehearsal suggestions assist with recital preparation. Designed to motivate your students with attainable goals, this comprehensively-leveled curriculum will make for phenomenal recital performances!

- **Musically engaging pieces by leading FJH composers and arrangers**

- **Original solos for recitals, contests and festivals**

- **Carefully leveled to ensure attainable goals—crucial in motivating students**

- **Recital repertoire for the entire year**

- **Solos and duets**

- **Variety of genres from classical music to jazz, blues, and rags to Christmas**

- **Performance strategies and rehearsal suggestions**

Companion CD included

In Recital® Throughout the Year, Volume One

In Recital® Throughout the Year, Volume Two

In Recital® with Christmas Favorites

In Recital® Duets

In Recital® with Classical Themes, Volume One

In Recital® with Jazz, Blues, & Rags

In Recital® with Popular Christmas Music

In Recital with... Satish Bhakta, Melody Bober, Timothy Brown, Kevin Costley, Martín Cuéllar, Lee Evans, Christopher Goldston, Elizabeth W. Greenleaf, David Karp, Nancy Lau, Mary Leaf, Edwin McLean, Emilie Lin, Helen Marlais, Kevin Olson, Wynn-Anne Rossi, Robert Schultz, Jason Sifford, Valerie Roth Roubos, and Judith R. Strickland.

Edited, compiled, and recorded by Helen Marlais

Segmented Bowls
FOR THE BEGINNING TURNER

Don Jovag

Schiffer Publishing Ltd

4880 Lower Valley Road • Atglen, PA 19310

Copyright © 2012 by Don Jovag

Library of Congress Control Number: 2012943240

Designed by Justin Watkinson
Type set in Agency FB/BaseTwelveSerif/Humanist 521 BT

ISBN: 978-0-7643-4165-6
Printed in China

Schiffer Books are available at special discounts for bulk purchases for sales promotions or premiums. Special editions, including personalized covers, corporate imprints, and excerpts can be created in large quantities for special needs. For more information contact the publisher:

Published by Schiffer Publishing Ltd.
4880 Lower Valley Road
Atglen, PA 19310
Phone: (610) 593-1777; Fax: (610) 593-2002
E-mail: Info@schifferbooks.com

For the largest selection of fine
reference books on this and related subjects,
please visit our website at **www.schifferbooks.com**
We are always looking for people to
write books on new and related subjects.
If you have an idea for a book, please contact us at
proposals@schifferbooks.com

This book may be purchased from the publisher.
Please try your bookstore first.
You may write for a free catalog.

In Europe, Schiffer books are distributed by
Bushwood Books
6 Marksbury Ave.
Kew Gardens
Surrey TW9 4JF England
Phone: 44 (0) 20 8392 8585; Fax: 44 (0) 20 8392 9876
E-mail: info@bushwoodbooks.co.uk
Website: www.bushwoodbooks.co.uk

Dedication

To my fine lady, Jeanne: without her assistance this book would never have been completed.

Contents

Preface

I love woodworking. And I love teaching. So it should be no surprise I was a high school woodworking teacher for thirty years in the public schools in the State of Washington. Of course, part of my teaching included turning bowls on the lathe. Like all novices on the lathe, my students had great difficulty when it came to turning end grain. That was no surprise. So did I. Since we often glued up pieces of wood into larger blocks to make our blanks for a bowl, it occurred to me, "How can we glue up some wood so we can eliminate turning end grain?" My experiment with making segmented bowls began!

Now, I know I'm not the first person to make segmented bowls. In fact, I found a limited amount of information on segmented bowls in some wood turning books and magazines. (Remember, this was before the Internet.) But, I knew that the information I had found was going to be much too complicated and/or frustrating for my high school students. I wanted to provide them with a segmented bowl project that would not only challenge them, but also fit their skill level and attention span. So, I set out to develop a segmented bowl project for my students. Over my years of teaching, I refined the process of making segmented bowls to the point that the "Segmented Bowl Project" became one of the most popular projects for my high school students.

Since retiring in 1995, I have moved to Arizona and now live in an active adult community. As it turns out, this community has a wonderful woodworking shop. My retirement gave me the opportunity to spend more time with woodworking in general, with the further development of my technique for making segmented bowls in particular. And, of course, my retirement also gave me the time to write this book.

I hope you will enjoy turning segmented bowls as much as I do. Each bowl offers a challenge all its own. As you become more experienced, you'll discover ways of making each bowl unique to you. Good luck and good turning.

Introduction

How to Use This Book

This book is intended to provide step-by-step instructions for making segmented bowls. I am directing my instruction to both the beginning wood turner as well as the more experienced turner. It is intended for those that have not yet attempted turning a segmented bowl, or for those that have tried but were not as successful as they would like to be. I have tried to explain each step in enough detail that a relatively inexperienced wood turner will be successful at making that first segmented bowl. At the same time, I think the more experienced wood turner will find making a segmented bowl a new challenge that he or she will appreciate.

Depending on your level of experience, you may already be familiar with some of the steps required in making a segmented bowl. My advice for you, the more experienced woodworker, would be to skim over each section, picking out and carefully reading the information that is new to you. On the other hand, the less experienced wood turner should pretty much follow along step-by-step.

Regardless of your experience level, pay close attention when you see a bold type **(Pay Attention!)** notation. I have made countless segmented bowls over the years, and countless mistakes to go with them. Some errors more than once! When I know I am describing a step that is particularly vulnerable to error, I have placed a **(Pay Attention!)** notice in the text. Obviously, no matter what your experience level is, you should really pay attention at this point. By the way, I would take it as a personal favor to me if you do not tabulate all of the mistakes I have made over the years. Counting up all of the **(Pay Attentions!)** you find in this book would be time consuming for you and embarrassing for me.

I am fortunate enough to be able to use a heavy duty Delta, Steel Bed™ lathe for turning bowls. It has a 16 inch swing and is reversible with an electronic variable speed. It is likely you may have a much smaller lathe, perhaps a mini lathe. If you are using a Jet-1014™ or Rikon 70-100™ or larger, you'll be fine. When using a mini lathe, you'll have to take a number of things into account to turn a successful bowl. I realized this and include extra precautions you must take when using a smaller, lighter weight lathe. When you see **mini lathe** in bold type in the text, it is an indication you will need to follow the precautions for lighter weight lathes with smaller accessories. Do not despair: you can make a very successful segmented bowl on lighter equipment than I use.

Overview of Segmented Bowls

The basic premise for making segmented bowls is simple. Instead of gluing up a square block of wood that you turn into a round bowl, you glue up a round, hollow shaped blank that you turn into a bowl. This offers a number of advantages. The biggest advantage to turning segmented bowls is that it virtually eliminates the problem of turning end grain. If you have ever tried turning a bowl from a solid block of wood, you know how difficult it is to turn and sand end grain. The end grain tends to chip out and sanding end grain to a smooth surface seems to be nearly impossible. By using segments to glue up a bowl blank, you will only be turning edge grain, and sanding is a pleasure. Well, at least it's not the drudgery of sanding chipped end grain. Plus, gluing up the segmented rings results in a blank that is already a hollow bowl shape. You will not have to spend the time and effort of turning out the center of the bowl, to say nothing of the wasted wood.

You can also use up a lot of small pieces of scrap wood to make your segments. All of us wood workers have hardwood scraps that we cannot bear to throw away. Except for the bottom, the entire bowl can be made from small pieces of wood. The only requirement is that these scrap pieces should be close to the same thickness.

Since you're gluing up the bowl blank from a lot of small pieces of wood, it is also easy to incorporate a design in the body of the bowl. The key to making a design is that all of the designs are a combination of different types of wood (color) and varying the length and alignment of the segments. By using either 12 or 24 segments in a ring, using different colors of wood, and by shifting the segmented rings in relationship to each other, you can create a number of different designs without the use of complicated jigs and fixtures for sanding, shaping, cutting, and gluing.

Of course, you could use rings with a different number of segments. The only requirement is that each ring must have an even number of segments. With an even number of segments, you can make half rings that are easy to fit and glue together into full rings. I use either 12 or 24 segments to a ring because of the relative ease of determining the angles that are required for making the fixtures that I use for cutting segments. Of course, the number of segments in each ring will determine the length and the miter angle that you must use to cut the segments. I will discuss this in more detail later in this book.

There are disadvantages associated with making segmented bowls. Segmented bowls require a lot of careful planning and accurate cutting and gluing. This is time consuming. But, I believe the advantages outweigh the time required to plan, cut, and glue-up a segmented bowl. Look at it as a new adventure when turning on the lathe. I think you will find it both interesting and challenging.

Tools Required

There is an extensive list of tools required for making segmented bowls.

Often a lathe is one of the last tools added to a wood shop, so if you have a lathe, you may already have the other tools necessary to make a segmented bowl. The following tool list is what I believe will make this effort the most efficient. Of course, there may be other tools you can substitute in place of those on the list. Since it is best to use lumber that has been "squared," it will require at a minimum a table saw, jointer, and a thickness planer if you are squaring the lumber yourself. However, if you have a source of squared lumber you only need a table saw for ripping to width and cutting segments to length. Making the primary and secondary designs for the bottom of a platter will require access to a jointer and a planer. For the purposes of this list, I will include all of them.

TOOL LIST

1. Table saw
2. Jointer
3. Thickness planer
4. Lathe with a minimum of a 10" swing
5. Drum thickness sander
6. Edge sander or disc sander
7. Band saw
8. Minimum of 6 to 8 large C-clamps or furniture clamps
9. Circle compass
10. Straight edge
11. An eight inch 30-60-90 degree and a twelve inch 45-45-90 degree mechanical drawing triangles
12. Your choice of lathe tools

CHAPTER 1
Salad Bowls

1-1:
Planning a Salad Bowl

To make the following instructions consistent, I'm going to describe the necessary steps for making a 9" diameter "L" shaped salad bowl. It will be nine inches in diameter because it will fit on a lathe with a 10" swing; an "L" shape because it is the easiest segmented bowl to make; and a salad bowl because it has a practical use. An "L" shaped bowl means the bowl blank will have rings of all the same diameter. Therefore, all the segments will be the same length. The intersection of the bottom and the straight up and down sides will form an "L." When you turn it on the lathe you will not leave the sides straight up and down, but instead give the bowl a more rounded "bowl" shape.

Decorator bowls are more difficult as each ring will be a different diameter and therefore the segments forming each ring will be a different length. Don't despair: I will also be discussing how to make a decorator bowl later in this book.

The first step is to determine the size and shape of the bowl. Since I have already determined we are going to make a 9" salad bowl with an "L" shape, let's look at the profile drawing below in Figure 1-1.

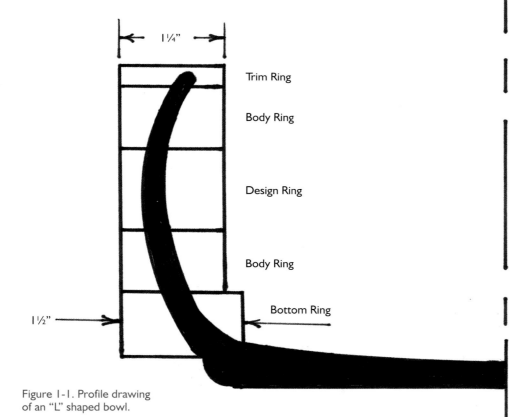

1¼"

Trim Ring

Body Ring

Design Ring

Body Ring

Bottom Ring

1½"

Figure 1-1. Profile drawing of an "L" shaped bowl.

As you can see, the distance from the centerline to the outside of the profile is 4-1/2", which will result in a 9" diameter bowl. The profile has the intended shape of the bowl, but it is basically straight up and down. As stated above, the intersection of the bowl side and the bottom form an "L," hence the "L" shape description. In the drawing, the rectangles you see are showing the ends of the segments (as if the bowl has been cut in half) used to form the rings. The profile drawing shows that the bowl will have a 1-1/2" wide bottom ring, two 1-1/4" wide body rings, a set of design rings and a top trim ring, also 1-1/4" wide. A detailed description on how to make each of these rings will follow.

The diameter of the bowl determines the length of each segment. To find the length of a segment we need to draw a 9" diameter circle and use geometry to draw an exact top view of one segment. Yes, I said geometry! Remember back in Geometry class in high school when you were sitting there thinking, "I'll never use this stuff in my life." Well, it shows you how much you knew! Here's your chance to use that geometry you learned in high school. With the use of some basic geometry techniques, you can easily determine the size of the segments for any segmented bowl you choose to make. Please don't despair: I will describe each step of the process with both words and pictures.

Figure 1-3. Starting anywhere on the circle, mark off one radius.

You will remember from geometry class that you can divide the perimeter of a circle into six equal parts by using a compass set to the radius of the circle. By starting at any point on the circle, mark off one 4-1/2" radius. (If you wish, you may want to mark off the radius 6 times around the perimeter of the circle which will prove that each marked off radius is one sixth of the circle). You only really need to mark off one radius so we have two adjacent points on the circle.

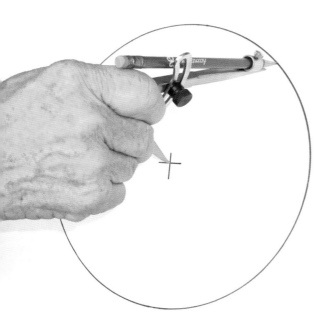

Figure 1-2. Drawing a 9"circle.

Using a compass set to 4-1/2", draw a 9" diameter circle.

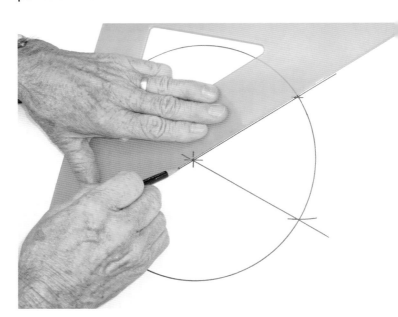

Figure 1-4. Drawing lines from the center of the circle through the two adjacent radii marked on the circle.

Draw a line from the center of the circle through these two adjacent points. Draw these lines about an inch out past the circle. This gives you a pie shape that represents one sixth of the circle. Accuracy is of the utmost importance. Be sure to draw these lines through the exact center of the circle and each of the two adjacent marks.

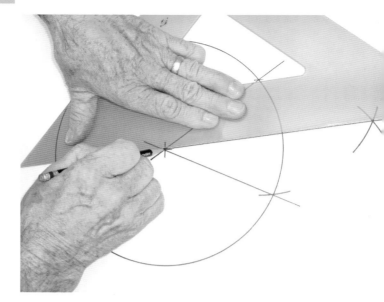

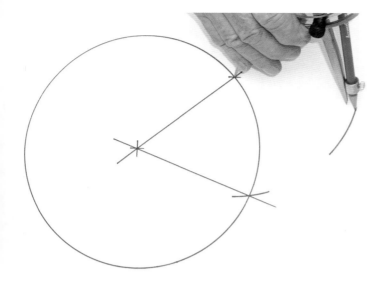

Figure 1-5. Striking the first arc to begin the bisection of the angle.

Figure 1-7. Drawing a line from the center of the circle through the point where the two arcs intersect.

Since you need one twelfth of the circle (we are trying to determine the size of one segment for a 12 segment ring), you will use geometry to bisect the angle you just drew. To do this, you don't even have to reset your compass. Place the point of your compass where one of the straight lines intersects the circle and draw an arc outside of the circle and between the two straight lines.

Draw a straight line from the center of the circle through the point where the two arcs intersect. Remember accuracy is important.

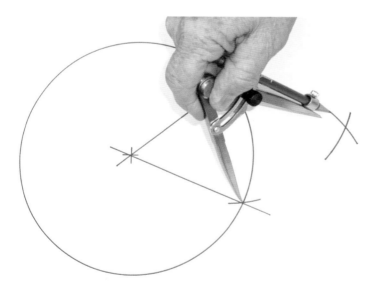

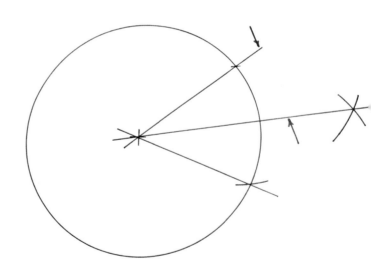

Figure 1-8. The bisection of the angle is complete.

Figure 1-6. Striking the second arc so it intersects with the first.

Without changing the compass setting, place the point of the compass on the other straight line where it intersects the circle and draw a second arc that intersects the first.

You have now bisected the angle that formed one sixth of the circle. This results in three lines forming two pie-shaped angles. Each pie-shaped angle represents one twelfth of the circle. We are only going to use two of these lines. Let's use the one in the middle and the line on the left. Note that these two lines are indicated by the arrows in Figure 1-8.

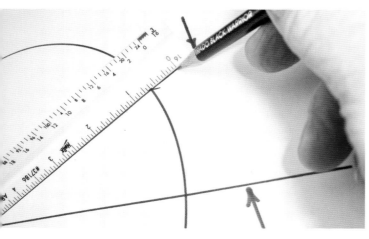

Figure 1-9. Measuring out from the circle 5/8".

Starting at the circle, measure out (away from the center of the circle) 5/8" along the line on the left. Draw a mark at this point. Measure out 5/8" along the middle of the three lines and draw a mark.

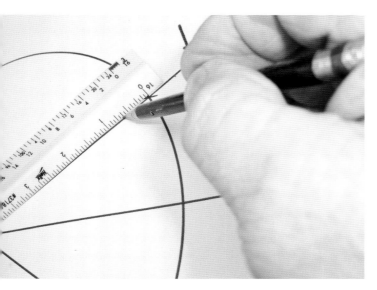

Figure 1-10. Measuring in from the circle 5/8".

Likewise, starting at the circle again, measure in (toward the center of the circle) 5/8" along the same two lines and draw a mark.

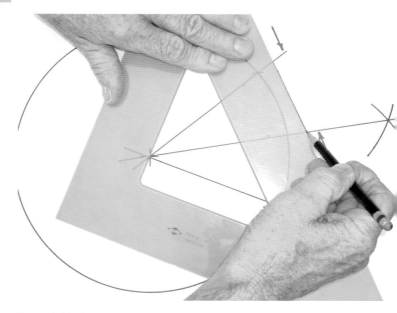

Figure 1-11. Connecting the marks with a straight line.

Now connect the marks both outside of the circle and inside of the circle.

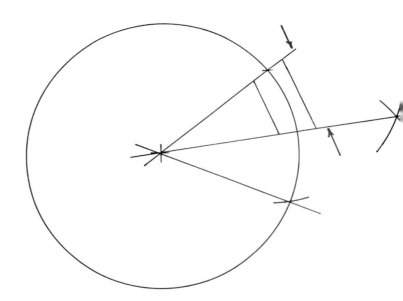

Figure 1-12. Connecting the four marks will result in a full size top view of one segment.

These two lines and the two lines that form one twelfth of the circle now show you the exact size and shape of the segment you need to make your bowl. In other words, you have just drawn an exact top view of the segments you need to cut.

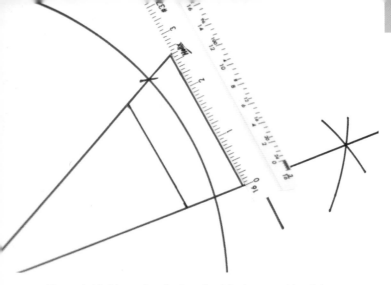

Figure 1-13. Measuring the length of the longest side of the segment.

You can now find the length of the segment you need to cut by measuring the length of the line outside of your circle. In the example of a 9" bowl we are making, it should be about 2-5/8" long. If your measurement is not close to 2-5/8", go back and check your work for accuracy.

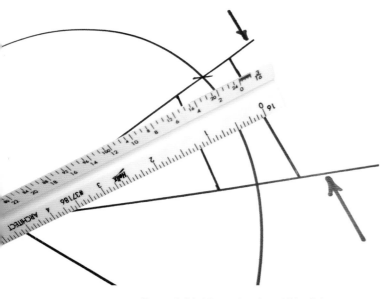

Figure 1-14. Measuring the width of the segment.

Measure the width of the segment you have drawn. It should be about 1-1/4" wide.

You should note that the bottom ring will be 1-1/2" wide. The extra width is to allow for the rabbet joint you will cut into this bottom ring. Not to worry, you do not have to redraw the segment for the wider bottom ring; just use 1-1/2" wide stock when cutting the bottom 12 segments. **(Pay Attention!)** When you're cutting the segments for the bottom ring, you must make sure all of the segments have the same 2-5/8" length along the longest side. That means you'll need to change the position of the stop block when you switch from the 1-1/2" stock to the 1-1/4" stock. Not to worry, more about that later in the section on cutting segments.

Since some designs also use rings that have 24 segments, you will have to cut these segments at a different miter angle and, of course, shorter. Logic tells us, if the segments that make up the 12 segment ring are 2-5/8" long, the segments that make up a 24 segment ring must be half the length. That's true. Therefore, the segments needed for a 24 segment ring will be 1-5/16" long. There is no need to draw a top view of a segment that represents one twenty fourth of the 9" circle. Just make sure that you cut them at half the length of the segments in a 12 segment ring. Cutting all segments accurately will result in all of the rings being the same diameter. **(Pay Attention!)** The diameter of each ring is determined by the length of the segments in the ring. The segments are very length specific. Cutting segments even 1/32" too long can add a 1/2" or more to the diameter of the ring. Cutting the half segments too long will result in the 24 segment rings not matching the 12 segment rings in diameter. It is essential that you cut the length of your segments accurately.

Figure 1-15. One of many possible designs for segmented bowls.

1-2:
Making Design Rings

As I stated before, the key to making the design is that all of the designs are a combination of different types of wood (color) and either 12 and/or 24 segments. By using different colors of wood and shifting the segmented rings in relationship to each other, you can create a number of different designs.

At the end of this book (Appendix A), you will find photos of a number of completed design rings and the number of segments required to make each design. Of course, you may make up your own designs by drawing them and counting the segments required. For the purpose of this book, I have selected the design that is shown in Figure 1-15. The following instructions will be used for making this design.

To cut the segments so they will glue up into a complete circle, you must calculate the miter angle for cutting the ends of the segments. To find this angle, you must divide the number of degrees in a circle (360 degrees) by the number of segments in a ring. In a 12 segment ring, 360 divided by 12 equals 30 degrees. Half of 30 degrees is 15 degrees (you must cut each end at half the angle you want), which will result in a 12-sided geometric figure. For 24 segments in a ring, the miter angle will be 7.5 degrees. 360 degrees divided by 24 equals 15 degrees. Half of 15 degrees is 7.5 degrees. Obviously, if you're making a ring with a different number of segments, you will have to calculate the correct miter angle. Just make sure you use an even number of segments in each ring. The reason for this requirement will become quite clear when you glue up the half rings into full rings.

The reason I use 12 and 24 segments to a ring is that it is easy to make cutting fixtures for your table saw for both the 15 and 7.5 degree miter angles by using common geometry techniques. Yes, I said *geometry* again! Not to worry, I will describe in detail how to make these fixtures later in this book.

For the bowl we are making, let's list the number of segments we will need. All of the segments will be 1-1/4" wide, **except** for the bottom ring. The rings are listed starting with the top ring and working down.

Top trim ring, which is also the first body ring, 12 segments of Padauk, about 3/8" thick by 1-1/4" wide.
Second body ring, 12 segments of Eastern Maple, about 3/4" thick by 1-1/4" wide.
Design rings that, when glued together, make up the third body ring:

    Top trim ring, 12 segments of Padauk, about 1/8" thick by 1-1/4" wide.
    Top spacer ring, 12 segments of Eastern Maple, about 1/8" thick by 1-1/4" wide.
    Top design ring, 24 segments, 12 of Padauk, 12 of Eastern Maple, about 1/4" thick by 1-1/4" wide.
    Middle design ring, 12 segments, 6 of Padauk, 6 of Eastern Maple, about 1/4" thick by 1-1/4" wide.
    Bottom design ring, 24 segments, 12 of Padauk, 12 of Eastern Maple, about 1/4" thick by 1-1/4" wide.
    Bottom spacer ring, 12 segments of Eastern Maple, about 1/8" thick by 1-1/4" wide.
    Bottom trim ring, 12 segments of Padauk, about 1/8" thick by 1-1/4" wide.

Fourth body ring, 12 segments of Eastern Maple, about 3/4" thick by 1-1/4" wide.
Bottom ring, 12 segments of Eastern Maple, about 3/4" thick **by 1-1/2" wide**.

Obviously, you need to keep track of the number of segments and the thickness, width, and length that you need to cut for each ring. So let's list all the segments we need by type of wood and their size.

Eastern Maple

24 at 3/4" by 1-1/4" by 2-5/8" (two body rings)
24 at 1/8" by 1-1/4" by 2-5/8" (two spacer rings)
12 at 3/4" by 1-1/2" by 2-5/8" (bottom ring)
6 at 1/4" by 1-1/4" by 2-5/8"
    (half of middle 12 segment design ring)
24 at 1/4" by 1-1/4" by 1-5/16"
    (part of the two 24 segment design rings)

Padauk

12 at 3/8" by 1-1/4" by 2-5/8" (top trim ring)
24 at 1/8" by 1-1/4" by 2-5/8" (two design trim rings)
6 at 1/4" by 1-1/4" by 2-5/8"
    (half of middle 12 segment design ring)
24 at 1/4" by 1-1/4" by 1-5/16"
    (part of the two 24 segment design rings)

Wow! That's a total of 156 individual segments. I know what you're thinking, "It's going to take forever to cut that many segments." Not really, especially if you use a sliding cutoff table. So, let's build one.

1-3:
Building a Sliding
Cutoff Table

Here is a list of the materials required to build your own sliding cutoff table. You will note the secondary fence is made of pine and the primary fence is made of a good grade of hardwood. I recommend Oak or Eastern Maple. We use hardwood for the primary fence because it acts as a chip breaker. A soft wood like Pine will erode away too fast to be a chip breaker.

    1/2" by 18" by 24" piece of good grade plywood, preferably hardwood veneer.
    Two 1-3/4" by 5" by 24" solid stock for primary and secondary fences. Softwood (Pine) is fine for the secondary fence, but use hardwood (Red Oak or Eastern Maple) for the primary fence.
    Two 3/8" by 3/4" by 18" Oak solid stock for table slot runners.
    12 number 8 by 1-3/4" flat head screws.
    10 number 8 by 3/4" flat head screws.

Figure 1-16. Attaching the secondary fence to the plywood base.

Start by making sure both the primary and secondary fences are square. This is to assure that the bottom edges are both straight and at a 90 degree angle to their faces. Install the secondary fence (pine) parallel to back the edge of 1/2" plywood base using the 1-3/4" screws. The attachment of the secondary fence to the plywood base does not require any accuracy. Its only function is to hold the plywood together once you cut the saw kerf into it. **(Pay Attention!)** Be sure you do not install a screw in the path of the blade.

Figure 1-17. Attaching the table slot runners to the plywood base with 3/4" screws.

With the table saw blade all the way down, place the plywood base (with the secondary fence attached) on the table saw with its front edge even with the front edge of the saw. You are not concerned about accuracy at this point; that will come later. Slide the 3/8" by 3/4" table slot runners into the table slots and under the plywood base. Mark the location of the center of each table slot runner on the plywood base. Use a square to draw a line on the center of each table slot runner from the front to the back on the plywood base. Using this line as a guide, drill pilot and clearance holes through the plywood base and into the table slot runners. Attach the table slot runners to the base using 3/4" screws.

Leaving the blade all the way down, make sure that the cutoff table slides back and forth smoothly. **(Pay Attention!)** It should slide smoothly with not too much effort. If it does not, there may be two reasons for this problem. First, you may just need to wax the table saw table with a good quality paste wax to reduce the friction. After waxing it may slide just fine. Or second (and more likely), you may have drilled pilot holes that are too small in diameter for the screws you used to attach the plywood base to the solid stock table slot runners. If the pilot holes are too small in diameter, driving in the screws may have split or expanded the oak runners to the extent they are wider than the 3/4" table slots. Adjust and repair as necessary.

Figure 1-19. Stop the cut about 2" from the edge of the plywood.

You will cut a saw kerf through the secondary fence and the plywood base. **(Pay Attention!)** Stop the cut about 2" from the edge of the plywood. In other words, do not cut the plywood base all the way through.

Figure 1-18. Cutting the saw kerf into the secondary fence and plywood base.

Once the cutoff table is sliding smoothly, cut a saw kerf in the plywood base by raising the blade of the table saw and slide the plywood base through the blade. Have your best carbide tooth crosscut blade on your table saw. The blade you plan to use when cutting the segments. **(Pay Attention!)** I recommend an eighty tooth carbide crosscut blade. Using a high quality crosscut blade will allow you to make precise cuts that will not require sanding before the segments are glued together.

Figure 1-20. Solid stock inserted into the saw kerf.

Machine a piece of solid stock so it will "friction fit" into the saw kerf you cut into the plywood base. It must fit tight so it identifies the exact location of the saw kerf.

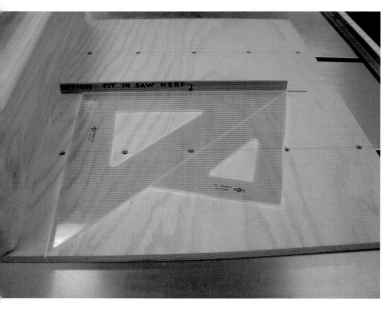

Figure 1-21. Triangles in place for drawing the 15 degree angle line.

Lay one of the short edges of a 45/45/90 degree mechanical drawing triangle against the solid stock in the saw kerf. With the 30 degree point of the 30/60/90 degree triangle pointing toward you, lay it against the 45 degree edge of the 45/90 degree triangle. The resulting angle on the lower edge of the 30/60/90 degree triangle will be 15 degrees to the saw kerf.

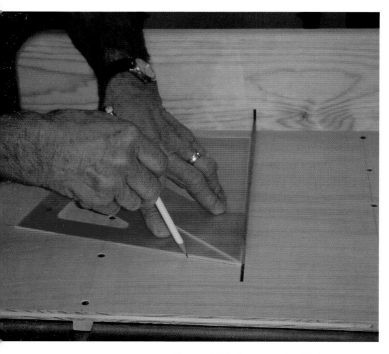

Figure 1-22. Drawing the 15 degree angle.

Just what you need! Using a sharp pencil, draw a line on the plywood base along the lower edge of the 30/60/90 degree triangle.

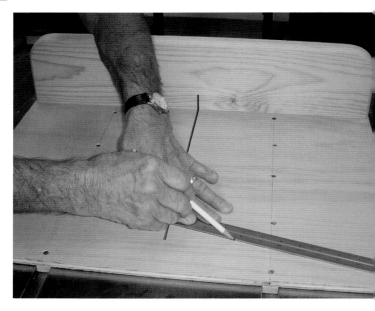

Figure 1-23. Extending the 15 degree angle line all the way across the plywood base.

Then, use a straight edge to extend this line all the way across the entire width of the plywood base.

Figure 1-24. Clamping the secondary fence even with the 15 degree angle line.

Next, carefully clamp the edge of the hardwood primary fence to the 15 degree line you just drew.

Figure 1-25. Attaching the 15 degree angle primary fence.

With the clamps firmly in place, remove the sliding cutoff table from the table saw. Make sure the primary fence is still even with the 15 degree line and attach it to the plywood base using 1-3/4" screws. Make sure you do not install a screw in line with the saw kerf.

Figure 1-26. Cutting the saw kerf through the rest of the plywood base and the primary fence.

Place the sliding cut off table back on the table saw. Start the saw and raise the blade. Finish cutting the saw kerf all the way through the secondary fence, the plywood base, and the 15 degree angle primary fence. You now have a 15 degree cut off table for cutting segments for a 12 segment ring.

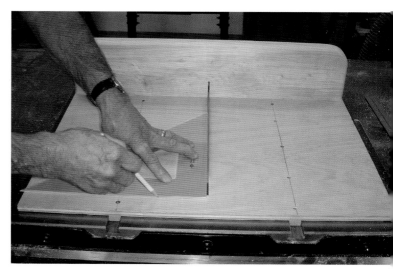

Figure 1-27. Drawing a 90 degree line to the saw kerf.

Making the 7-1/2 degree cutoff table requires the same steps. You must establish a 15 degree angle that you will then bisect. Start with a new set of materials and follow the same steps up through cutting the saw kerf. At this point you must establish a line at a 90 degree angle to the saw kerf. As you did before, cut the saw kerf in the plywood base, stopping about 2" from the edge. Place the friction fit solid stock piece into the saw kerf. Use the 45/45/90 degree triangle to draw a line on the plywood base at a 90 degree angle to the saw kerf.

Figure 1-28. Drawing the 15 degree angle.

Using both triangles again, draw a line at 15 degrees so it intersects with the 90 degree line you just drew.

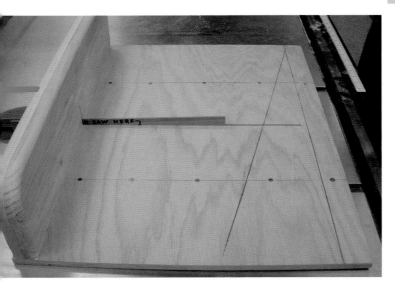

Figure 1-29. The 15 degree angle ready to be bisected.

When you're finished drawing both lines, you'll have a 15 degree angle that you must now bisect.

Figure 1-30. Striking an arc is the first step of bisecting the 15 degree angle.

Using the same geometric construction techniques you used to bisect the 30 degree angle when you were drawing a picture of a segment, bisect the 15 degree angle you drew on the plywood base. Start by placing the compass point on the intersection of the 90 degree line and the 15 degree line and strike a large arc.

Figure 1-31. Striking the second of two arcs required to bisect the 15 degree angle.

Now place the compass point on the intersection of the arc you just drew and the line that is at a 90 degree angle to the saw kerf. Strike an arc between the two lines that form the 15 degree angle. Strike a second arc with the compass point on the 15 degree line.

Figure 1-32. Close up of the intersection of the two arcs.

As you can see in Figure 1-32, the exact intersection between the two arcs may be hard to determine. You must carefully mark what appears to be exact point that the two arcs cross each other. Once you have determined that point, check yourself. Measure from each of the lines that form the 15 degree angle to the point you marked as the intersection of the two arcs. Both measurements **must** be the same.

Figure 1-33. Drawing the 7-1/2 degree angle line.

After finding the point of exact intersection of the two arcs, use a straight edge to draw a line from the apex of the 15 degree angle and the intersection point.

Figure 1-34. The completed bisection of the 15 degree angle provides a 7-1/2 degree line.

With the bisection complete, we now have a 7-1/2 degree angle line that establishes the location of the primary fence. As you did before when making the 15 degree cut off table, clamp the primary fence to the plywood base along the 7-1/2 degree line. Attach the primary fence to the plywood base with 1-3/4" screws. I would advise you to make a 90 degree cutoff table too. Make it a little larger than the 15 and 7-1/2 degree cutoff tables. The plywood base should be about 24" by 36". Of course both fences would have to be 36" long too. It is made by using the same procedure that was used in making the 15 and 7-1/2 degree cutoff tables. This time you'll set the primary fence at a 90 degree angle to the saw kerf. Cut the saw kerf in the plywood base stopping

short by two inches. Place the friction fit piece in the saw kerf as you did for the other sliding cut off tables. Place a framing square or a 12 inch 45/45/90 mechanical drawing triangle against the friction fit piece in the saw kerf. Clamp the primary fence to the plywood base, using the triangle or square to assure it is exactly at a right angle to the saw kerf. Screw the primary fence to the base, finish cutting the saw kerf through the primary fence, and you're done. Note that only screws are used to fasten the wooden parts of the cutoff tables together. After years of use, the cutoff tables will eventually wear out. By only using screws to fasten them together, they can easily be rebuilt.

While you do not need a 90 degree cutoff table for making the typical segments for most segmented bowls, you will find it so "handy" for all kinds of 90 degree crosscutting, you will not know how you got along without one. You might as well build all three at the same time and save a lot of duplicated effort.

1-4: Machining the Stock and Cutting Segments

Accuracy is very important when you are cutting segments. When using solid stock lumber, you must square the material to eliminate twists and/or bows in the lumber. Using scrap material requires machining all of your pieces of scrap to the same thickness and width. In any case, the more accurate the better. Accuracy allows the segments to easily fit together during the gluing process and the half rings will fit together with less error.

I am going to assume that you have made a sliding cutoff table to cut your segments. I'm assuming this because I believe that using the sliding cutoff table results in the most efficient and accurate way to cut segments. You could also cut segments with a "chop saw" or compound miter saw or even a miter gauge on a table saw. With today's digital protractors, these saws may be set up with great accuracy. But that is also a problem: the set up. Every time you need to cut segments, you would have to set up the saw all over again. With a sliding cutoff table, you set it up once; when you make it. (Note: The chop saw or compound miter saw also require three hands to cut segments; one hand to hold the segment, a second to operate the saw, and a third to hold down the solid stock). Obviously, you would have to rig up a clamping system to hold the solid stock which adds to the set up time. While you may use an alternative method to cut segments, I will be using the sliding cutoff table in my instructions and photos in this book.

Before cutting any segments, install a good crosscut blade on your table saw. An 80 tooth carbide crosscut blade would be best. **(Pay Attention!)** It is critical to make a smooth, even cut on both ends of each segment. This is to assure the best possible joint between segments.

No matter what method or machine you use to cut your segments, you start off by cutting one end of your solid stock at the required angle. When cutting segments for a 12 segment ring, cut them at 15 degrees. After making the first 15 degree miter cut, measure from the end of the solid stock and draw a mark at the required length for the segments you are cutting. In the example of the 9" diameter bowl, your mark will be at 2-5/8". When using a sliding cut off table, cut a stop block at the same 15 degree angle and place it on the 15 degree cutoff table against the fence and to the right of the blade. Turn the solid stock over and slide it along the fence of the cutoff table until it is in contact with the stop block. Adjust the stop block so the blade of your table saw will cut the solid stock at the mark you drew on your wood at the distance of 2-5/8". Clamp the stop block in place and cut your first segment. You do this by first pushing the cutoff table away from you, cutting the segment, and then pulling the cutoff table back (toward you) through the cut.

Figure 1-36. Note that there is a gap between the two segments due to the table saw blade being at a slight angle (other than 90 degrees) to the top of the table.

After you have cut one segment and removed it from the cutoff table, you turn over the solid stock and slide it against the 15 degree stop block. Cut a second segment. **(Pay Attention!) STOP** cutting segments at this point. Take the two segments you have cut and place them on a flat surface and hold their ends tightly together to see if they match (join) perfectly. You're looking for a "perfect fit," with the top to bottom having no gaps. You're checking to see that they fit for the gluing process to follow. If there is a poor fit, it typically is due to the table saw blade not being at a perfect 90 degree angle to the saw's table.

Figure 1-35. Use a pencil eraser to hold the segment while cutting.

It is too dangerous to hold the segment down with your fingers, so hold it down with a pencil eraser as shown in Figure 1-35. **(Pay Attention!)** It is absolutely essential that you firmly support the segment during this cutting operation. If the segment is allowed to move, it may "hop" or vibrate. This is especially true when you pull the cutoff table back through the cut. Any vibration of the segment may result in the face of the cut not being precise enough for accurate gluing later. Your goal is to cut the segments with enough precision to allow accurate gluing without having to "touch up" the faces.

Figure 1-37. A perfect fit between the ends of the two segments.

Adjust the blade and cut two more segments and check for a perfect fit again. Once you are satisfied you're getting a perfect fit, continue cutting segments until you have the number of 15 degree segments you need for the body, trim, spacer, and design rings for your bowl.

Start by cutting segments for the bottom ring first. As we have determined, the bottom ring will require cutting 12 segments 2-5/8" long by 1-1/2" wide made out of approximately 3/4" thick stock. Next cut the segments for rings that require segments of 2-5/8" long and 1-1/4" wide. **(Pay Attention!)** You must **re-set the stop block on the cutoff table** before you cut these segments. Because you're now cutting narrower stock (1-1/4" instead of 1-1/2" wide), if you do not move the stop block your 1-1/4" wide segments will be too long. **(Pay Attention!)** This rule always applies: when you change the width of the segments you're cutting, you also have to change the location of the stop block to cut the required length.

You'll use the exact same method for cutting the segments for rings requiring 24 segments. Of course you must use a 7-1/2 degree cutoff table for these segments and cut them at half the length of the 15 degree segments. In the example we are using, the length of the 7-1/2 degree segments will be 1-5/16". Continue cutting segments until you have the required number for both the full length (12 to a ring) and half length (24 to a ring) segments.

1-5:
Friction Gluing Segments

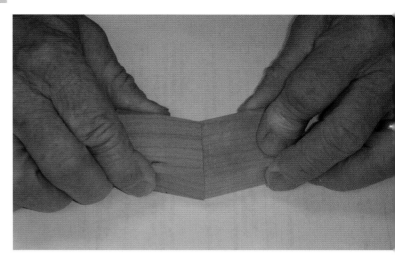

Figure 1-39. Friction gluing two segments together.

Figure 1-38. Sanding off the fuzzy edge.

The technique of "rub" or "friction" gluing will be used to join the segments together. Friction gluing requires a good clean end grain face to obtain the best result. Often the segments will have "fuzzy" edges at the intersection of the end grain end and the face grain (top and/or bottom) after they are cut. The amount of "fuzz" will depend on a number of factors. The density of the wood and the sharpness of the blade are just two of the factors that determine how "clean" the cut will be on the ends of the segments. If some or all of the segments have fuzzy edges, you must sand off the fuzz prior to the gluing process. This will require placing a sheet of abrasive paper on your bench, holding the segment at a 45 degree angle, and sanding off the fuzz. **(Pay Attention!)** You are **not** sanding the ends of the segments. You are sanding the "point" of the intersection between the end grain and the face grain of the segment. If you sand the end of the segments, you'll likely change the angle of your miter cut or ruin the "clean" end of the segment. An 80 tooth carbide crosscut blade and the "chip breaking" action of a sliding cut off table is the best guard against having a fuzzy edge.

Using Tight Bond™ Type II glue, friction glue your segments together on a flat surface that is covered with waxed paper. "Rub" gluing or "friction" gluing is nothing new. It is a most convenient way of gluing each segment to the next without clamping. Using a glue bottle, apply a small line of glue to one end of a segment. Place the two segments you are gluing end to end on your flat surface and literally rub the two ends of the segments back and forth. With just a few back and forth strokes, you will realize that it will become noticeably more difficult to move them back and forth. At this point, make sure that the two segments are perfectly aligned the way you want them (ends lined up and flat) and just let go. Wipe off any excess glue that squeezes out on top of the two segments. If you have never used this "friction" glue technique before, you'll be amazed how quickly the glue joint becomes strong enough for you to pick up the two segments and complete the next gluing operation. **(Pay Attention!)** You'll be tempted to "dip" the end of a segment you are about to glue, in a puddle of glue instead of using a glue bottle. While it will be more efficient to apply glue this way, you'll apply an excessive amount as well. This will result in the segments sticking to the waxed paper and getting glue all over your fingers. In other words, it will become a real mess! Use a glue bottle.

This glue joint is an end grain to end grain butt joint, so it is not very strong. However, it is more than strong enough to withstand all of the following gluing and sanding operations. Just don't drop the rings on the floor; they will most likely break.

The bowl, however, will be very strong. What makes the bowl strong is you will eventually be gluing each ring to the one above and below it in a brick wall fashion. In other words, you will be gluing the rings together so each segment is glued to the two above it and the two below it. With each segment off-set by half, you end up with a lap joint for every segment. This, of course, is much stronger than the end grain butt joints used to glue the segments together.

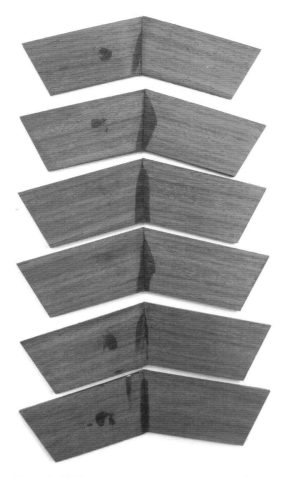

Figure 1-40. Twelve segments glued up in pairs for a trim ring.

When gluing up rings of 12, start by gluing all 12 of your segments in pairs of two.

Figure 1-41. Two pairs glued into fours with two pairs held out.

Then, glue the pairs of two into sets of four, but **(Pay Attention!)** hold out one pair of two for each set of four. The sets of four will then be glued to the pairs to make half rings of six segments each.

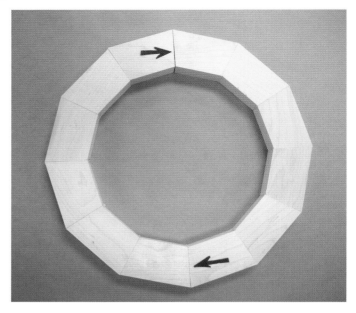

Figure 1-42. Arrows indicate a slight gap between the four ends of the two half rings in this body ring.

Glue the sets of four to the pairs of two to make half rings of six segments each. You will notice that the four ends of the two half rings will likely not be matched up well enough to glue the two half rings together. A small gap is typical. If all the rings have a larger gap of 1/8" or more, you may want to check the angle of the primary fence on your cutoff table. It may be that the primary fence needs to be adjusted to cut closer to the 15 degree angle required for cutting segments.

Figure 1-43. Sanding the two ends of a half ring into the same plane.

Use an edge or disc sander to sand the two ends of the half rings into the same plane. Sand one half ring with one face down on the table and sand the other half ring with the opposite face down on the table. Sanding with opposite faces down on the table compensates for the possibility the table is not set exactly at 90 degrees to the face of the sander's surface. **(Pay Attention!)** Obviously you'll be sanding the four ends only slightly, but they will be somewhat shorter than the rest of the segments. For body rings, this is not a critical problem; however, it may be for the design rings. Design rings form the design by the careful alignment of the different colors of wood. Sanding, even a small amount, may disrupt the design. For some designs it may require cutting the four end segments (two each for both half rings) to a slightly longer length. Keep track of these longer segments by drawing some sort of a mark on them. Then make sure they end up on the four ends of the two half rings. This longer length allows for the sanding of these four ends in the edge sander so they end up the same length as the rest of the segments. Most of the time, I compensate for the fact that these four ends are sanded slightly shorter by keeping track of them. In other words, I mark the location of the glue joints of the two half rings that form the full ring. Then, as I align the rings to form the design, I keep them together in the same location in the design. Most of the time this works well enough. As you begin to make more precise designs, your experience will tell you if just marking the glue joint of the half rings is enough or if cutting these four segments slightly longer is required to facilitate your design.

Figure 1-44. Two half rings glued together into one complete ring.

Rub glue the half rings of six into full rings of twelve.

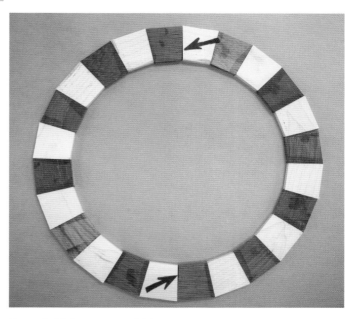

Figure 1-45. Design ring of 24 segments. Arrows indicate the gap between the half rings that will need to be edge sanded into the same plane before gluing into a full ring.

When gluing up rings of 24, glue all your segments into pairs of two. Next glue the pairs of two into sets of four. Then glue the sets of four into sets of eight, but (**Pay Attention!**) for every set of eight, hold out a set of four. Glue the sets of eight to the sets of four to make half rings of twelve segments each. Use an edge sander or disc sander to sand ends into the same plane and rub glue the two half rings of twelve into a full ring of 24.

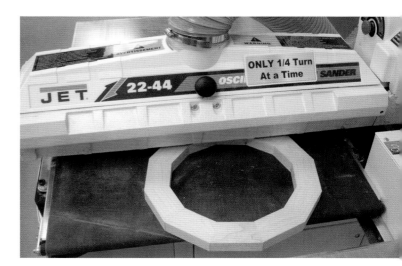

Figure 1-46. Running the rings through a thickness sander.

Once the rings are glued together, you will notice that they will not be smooth enough to glue one on top of another to form a hollow bowl shape. To solve this problem, run each ring through a drum thickness sander to smooth out the surfaces. Do not thickness sand the rings the same day you have completed the gluing, as the soft glue will clog up the abrasive paper on the drum sander.

1-6:
Gluing the Design Rings

At this point, I always glue up the design rings, also called feature rings, separately from the rest of the body rings. I do this for two reasons. First, it reduces the number of separate rings you must glue when gluing up the entire bowl. Second, most designs require that some, if not all, of the segments must be lined up in some way to complete the design. The problem is, when the rings are lubricated with glue, they will slip out of place and ruin the design alignment when clamp pressure is applied. To prevent this critical problem, we will "pin" the design in place with three 1/8" wood dowels. Wood dowels are used because they will be safely cut away and disappear during the turning process on the lathe.

Without applying any glue and using two C-clamps, carefully clamp the design plus the spacer and trim rings in place. Be sure to check for both design alignment and that the trim and spacer rings are in the proper "brick wall" alignment. It often takes several attempts to achieve perfect alignment. Check carefully, this is your one and only opportunity to get the design perfect. When you are satisfied all the rings are in proper alignment, tighten the two C-clamps.

Figure 1-47. Drilling the dowel holes with a 9/64" diameter drill.

Use a drill press to drill three 9/64" holes on the outer edge around the perimeter of the clamped up design rings. If you do not have a drill press, use a drill motor and drill the holes as vertically as possible.

Figure 1-48. Gluing up the design rings with the dowels in place.

Cut three 1/8" dowels just short of the thickness of the clamped up design rings. Cut two plywood discs approximately 10" in diameter to act as glue blocks. Tear off two pieces of waxed paper large enough to cover one side of each of the plywood discs. Unclamp the design rings but do not change their position. Lift the top trim ring off the stack of design rings and place it on top of one of the plywood discs that is covered with waxed paper. Insert the three dowels into the three holes in this ring and apply glue to this ring and the top ring on the stack of rings making up the design. Figure 1-48 shows the gluing process with the dowels in place.

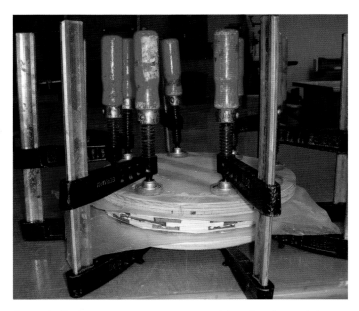

Figure 1-49. Clamping up the design rings. Note the plywood glue blocks with waxed paper in between.

Repeat this process until all the design rings are glued and pinned into place. With waxed paper in between the design rings and the plywood discs, use 6 to 8 clamps to complete the gluing of the design rings.

1-7:
Gluing Up the Bowl

Figure 1-51. Design rings cut to a 9-1/2"diameter circle. The arrow points to the wood dowel that was exposed when the design rings were cut into a circle.

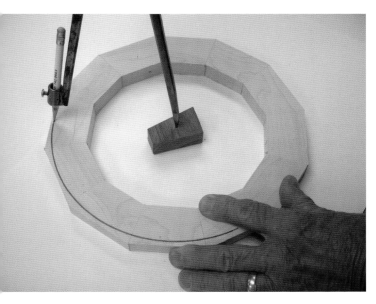

Figure 1-50. Drawing a 9-1/2" diameter circle on a completed ring. Note the block is attached to the bench with double-sided tape to elevate the compass point.

Once the design rings are out of the clamps, you are ready to glue up the rest of the rings to form the hollow bowl shape. Using a band saw cut all of the rings (including the glued up design rings) that form the body of the bowl into 9-1/2" diameter circles. Use a compass to draw the 9-1/2" circles on the rings, or cut a plywood disc with a 9-1/2" diameter and trace around it on each ring. When using a compass, you will probably need to use double-sided tape to fasten a wood block to your bench to elevate the point of the compass.

Cutting the rings into circles makes it much easier to glue them up on center, which of course results in better balance. Better balance provides for less vibration during the turning process. Cutting them into circles also eliminates the nerve racking turning off of "corners" on the 12 sided rings. If you do not have a band saw, it is not absolutely necessary to saw the rings into 9-1/2" circles. The bowl may be turned with all the "corners" left on the 12 and 24 sided rings. However, as I stated above, it is much easier to glue up and turn the bowl if all the rings are cut into circles. It would be best for **mini lathe** users to find a way to cut your rings into circles.

(Pay Attention!) Before starting the gluing process of the entire bowl, mark the location of the wood dowels both on the inside and outside of the design rings. By doing this, you will be able to keep track of their location while you are turning the rings. You want to be sure they are turned out of the bowl so they will not show in the final bowl shape. In many cases the dowels will appear during the process of cutting the design rings into a 9-1/2" circle on the band saw so you will already know their location.

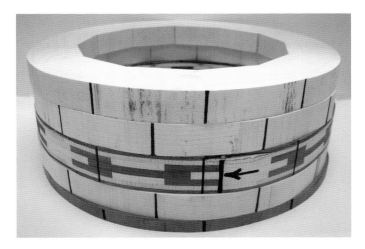

Figure 1-52. Rings are stacked up in order. Note the butt joints between segments have been marked to emphasize the correct brick-like configuration. The arrow indicates the location of one of the three wooden dowels used to "pin" the design rings during gluing.

After all the rings have been cut into circles, stack them up with the top trim ring on the bottom and the wider 1-1/2" ring (bottom ring) on the top. Notice the stack will be upside down from the finished bowl.

The order of the stack will be:
> Top trim ring on the bottom of the stack.
> Eastern Maple body ring.
> Glued-up design and trim rings.
> Eastern Maple body ring.
> 1-1/2" wide Eastern Maple bottom ring on top of the stack.

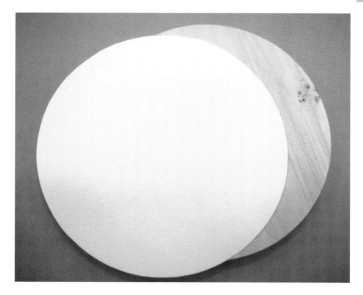

Figure 1-53. Plywood disc and the card stock that will be glued in between the plywood and the top trim ring.

Figure 1-54. Gluing up rings. Note the brick-like configuration of the segments.

(Pay Attention!) No glue has been applied yet. You have just stacked them up in the order as described above. Before starting to apply glue you will need to prepare a plywood faceplate and cut a circle out of 40 to 50 pound card stock paper. The plywood faceplate will need to be cut from 3/4" plywood at 9-1/2" in diameter. The paper circle must fit the plywood faceplate you have prepared. You can purchase card stock at your local office supply store. The card stock will be glued in-between the plywood faceplate and the top trim ring, which is now the bottom ring in your stack.

A metal faceplate will be attached to the plywood faceplate with screws. The metal faceplate will be mounted on the lathe for turning the bowl. The card stock will allow you to remove the plywood faceplate from the trim ring after you have turned the bowl round and cut the rabbet joint for the bottom. You will see how to remove the plywood face plate later.

If you will be turning your bowl on a **mini lathe** and you do not have a 6" diameter metal faceplate, double the thickness of your false plywood faceplate. Most of the smaller metal faceplates have only four holes for the attachment screws. That is not enough to withstand the forces of turning the bowl. Four screws will likely pull out if they are too short. By doubling the thickness of the plywood faceplate you will be able to use longer screws and avoid this problem.

Take the bottom ring off the top of your stack, turn it over and apply glue. Apply glue to the next ring, take it off the stack, turn it over and place it on the bottom ring being careful to align it in a brick-like fashion. Notice you are applying glue to both surfaces of each ring being glued. Continue until you have applied glue to each ring and aligned it properly. **(Pay Attention!)** Make sure the stack of rings is straight up and down and the end grain joints are in the brick wall configuration. Be sure to apply glue to the top trim ring and the plywood faceplate. Also

be sure to slip the card stock in between the top trim ring and plywood faceplate. Make sure the plywood faceplate is on center with the rings. Place another plywood disc on the bottom of your stack. **Do not apply glue to this second plywood disc:** it is just a glue block. Using 6 to 8 large furniture clamps or C-clamps, apply pressure to your stack of rings. Make sure the rings do not slip out of alignment, both in their straight up and down position and their brick wall configuration. **Mini lathe** users should be extra careful to glue the rings on center. As stated before, gluing any of the rings off center will result in excessive vibration, which will be a greater problem on lighter lathes.

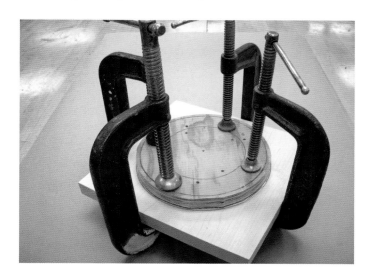

Figure 1-55. Plywood faceplate being glued to the Eastern Maple stock that eventually will become the bottom of the bowl. Card stock is glued in between.

While you are waiting for the glue to cure, it is time to make the bottom of the bowl. If you don't have a piece of Eastern Maple at least 9" wide, glue up an approximately 9" square for the bottom. Cut a round disc out of 3/4" plywood about 6" to 7" in diameter. This will be another false faceplate for the bottom of the bowl. **Mini lathe** users with a 3 or 4 inch diameter faceplate need to again double the thickness of the false plywood faceplate to accommodate longer screws. Glue the plywood disc to the exact center of the Eastern Maple bottom with card stock in-between. To do this, find the center of the Eastern Maple square and draw a circle with your compass just slightly larger than the plywood faceplate. Apply glue inside the circle and on the plywood faceplate. Slip the card stock (which you have cut to the same size as the plywood faceplate) in between and apply pressure with clamps. Make sure the plywood does not slip outside of the circle you drew on the Eastern Maple. This bottom will be turned later into a perfectly round disc to fit into the rabbet joint you will cut in the bottom ring of the bowl.

You may wonder why we just don't glue this bottom right on to the rings and be done with it. That would certainly be easier than cutting and fitting the bottom into a rabbet joint. In fact, my first segmented bowls were made this way. I now use the rabbit joint for several reasons. First, it is very difficult to turn the bottom and the adjoining bottom ring into a pleasing curve. Plus trying to turn a "dish" into the bottom with the body of the bowl in the way is difficult. It is much easier to turn and sand the bottom by itself. There is also the matter of ascetics. I believe the bowl looks better with a "foot" to sit on. By gluing a bottom into a rabbet joint you provide a smaller, more delicate base.

1-8:
Tool Sharpening

Before we start turning our bowl, we need to select our tools and sharpen them. Tool sharpening always seems to be a difficult subject. Tool selection may be even more difficult. I use two tools when turning segmented bowls; a scraper to turn the body and a parting tool to cut the rabbet.

I do not sharpen the scraping tool in the usual way. Instead, I sharpen it to act more like a cutting tool than a scraper. As you see in Figure 1-56 and 1-57, I sharpen the

Figure 1-56. Side view of a sharpened scraper.

Figure 1-57. Top view of a sharpened scraper.

scraper at approximately a 30 degree angle with a hollow ground surface and a rounded tip.

I realize this is an unorthodox way of sharpening a scraping tool. I must confess that I'm mostly self-taught when it comes to turning on the lathe. I have experimented with various tools and sharpening techniques. I am satisfied with the results I obtain. Many of you will have your own technique for sharpening and tool selection. Use what works best for you.

Figure 1-58. This is typical of the type of shavings you should expect with a properly sharpened tool.

You are cutting edge grain only when turning a segmented bowl. In fact, as stated before, that is the primary advantage of turning segmented bowls. Since you are turning edge grain only, you should be getting long fluffy shavings like those in Figure 1-58. If not, resharpen your lathe tool.

Honing your lathe tool is a must! I hone my lathe tool on a Red India oil stone right after sharpening. While turning the bowl I frequently stop and hone the lathe tool to keep it sharp. I will hone the lathe tool a dozen or more times between each sharpening.

I normally use a vertical belt sander to sharpen the scraper. Keeping the scraper tool in contact with the upper roller area on the sander results in a hollow ground surface. **(Pay Attention!)** If you decide to use a vertical belt sander, as I do, disconnect it from the dust collection system. Sparks from sharpening, when mixed with wood dust, have the potential of causing an explosion and fire.

Whatever tool you use and whatever sharpening technique you use, a sharp tool always cuts best. Remember, you're trying to cut the wood away, not rub it off. There is no substitute for sharp tools!

Figure 1-59. Honing a lathe tool on a Red India oil stone.

1-9:
Turning the Bowl

Figure 1-60. Drawing a circle on the plywood faceplate slightly larger than the metal faceplate.

It is time to mount a 6" metal faceplate to the plywood faceplate.

Using a compass, place the point of the compass on the center of the plywood faceplate and draw a circle just slightly larger than the metal faceplate.

Figure 1-61. Attaching a metal faceplate to the plywood faceplate.

Locate the metal faceplate inside the circle you just drew. Mark the location of the holes and drill for the screws you're using to mount the metal faceplate to the plywood.

Make sure to check how far the screws extend out of the metal faceplate. Obviously, you do not want the screws to go all the way through the plywood faceplate. If the screws were to pierce the plywood they would be quite dangerous to your knuckles when turning deep into the bowl.

Remember, **mini lathe** users: if you're using a metal faceplate that has only four screw holes, double the thickness of the plywood faceplate so you can install it with longer screws.

Figure 1-62. Rings mounted on the lathe and ready to turn.

As you can see, you will be turning the rings with the top ring (which is glued to the plywood faceplate) closest to the head of the lathe and the bottom ring closest to you. Although it appears that you are turning the bowl upside down, eventually you will be turning the rabbet joint into the bottom ring to accept the bottom of the bowl. Once the bottom of the bowl is turned round and glued into the rabbet joint, you will finish turning the bowl right-side up, so to speak.

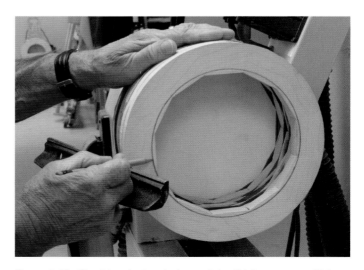

Figure 1-63. Checking the bowl, determining if it is on center. This bowl looks close enough to being on center to start turning it round.

Before you turn on the lathe, you'll want to check if your gluing job was reasonably accurate—that is, your rings are on center and reasonably close to being in balance. Set up the lathe's tool rest so you can hold a pencil steady enough to draw a circle on the bottom ring while turning the rings with your other hand. Draw this circle as close as possible to the inside edge of the segments on the bottom ring. If your glue job was dead-on accurate, the line will almost touch each point where the 12 segments meet.

It will be very unlikely that your glue job will be dead-on. It will be more likely that the line you draw will almost touch on one side of the bottom ring and will wander away from the segments on the other. This is the case in Figure 1-64. In fact, the line shows it to be about 1/2" off center. Typically, that is too far off center to try turning it without some sort of adjustment.

Figure 1-64. As you can see, this set of rings is off center. The line is right on the edge of the segments on the left side of the bowl and at least 1/2" off on the right.

How far it is off center will determine if you can turn the bowl as is, or if you have to adjust the location of the metal faceplate. So, how do you tell? First, if the line wanders off by much more than 3/8" from the inside edge of the segments, it may be too far out of balance to turn without an adjustment. Second, spin the glued up rings by hand and watch to see if the rings seem to "swing" way off center. Rings that appear to be way out of round (off center) when you spin them by hand, is an indication that the location of the metal faceplate may have to be adjusted. Third, and the most critical test, is to turn on the lathe and see what happens. **(Pay Attention!)** Before you start the lathe, make sure the lathe is set up to turn at a low RPM. Also, be ready to turn the lathe off immediately if necessary. In fact, if I'm not sure, I will switch the lathe on and then off quickly and observe what happens. If it seems alright, I will turn on the lathe for a few seconds and observe it again.

So, what are you looking for on this test? You're looking for vibration. Now, on almost every set of glued up rings you'll experience some vibration. On a heavy duty lathe, you may be able to turn the rings round without being concerned about a small amount of vibration. If the rings are too far off center, the lathe will start to vibrate to the extent that the lathe may start to "walk" across the floor. If this happens you will want to turn off the lathe and get out of the way! **Mini lathe** users will want to be very careful when preforming this third test! Because of their light weight, the "walking" of the lathe could be quite exciting.

In either case, heavy duty or mini lathe, the vibration may be too much to start turning the rings round. In this case, relocating the metal faceplate is a good place to start. The direction you must move the faceplate can be a bit confusing. The line you drew to check the alignment will give you a clue of which direction and how far to move the faceplate. Measure the amount the bottom ring is off center. In Figure 1-64, the rings are about 1/2" off center.

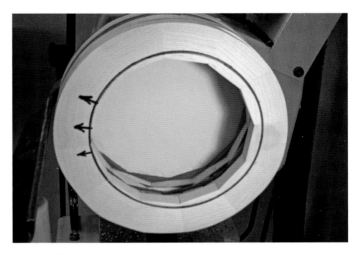

Figure 1-65. Arrows show the direction you want the circle to move.

Rotate the rings so the line closest to the edge of the segments is on the left. Draw a few arrows showing the direction you want the circle to move.

The arrows you drew point in the direction that you must move the metal faceplate. Since you must redraw the circle for the metal faceplate, you must find a new center point for your compass. The amount you move this center

Figure 1-66. Redrawing the circle for the metal faceplate using the new center. The red arrow indicates the old center.

point is about half the distance the line is away from the edge of the segments on the other side of the rings. In the example in Figure 1-65, this distance is about 1/2". Remove the rings from the lathe, and remove the screws holding the metal faceplate to the plywood faceplate. Mark a new center for the compass **at half the measured distance** and **in the direction of the arrows** on the bottom ring. In the example in Figure 1-65, the measured distance was 1/2", so you reset the center of the circle 1/4" from the old center. Draw another circle just slightly larger than your metal faceplate using this new center point. Install the metal faceplate and return the rings to the lathe.

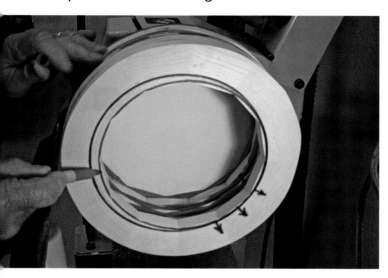

Figure 1-67. Using a red pen to check if moving the metal faceplate solved the problem of the off center rings.

Check if the bottom ring is closer to being on center. If it is, as in Figure 1-67, you are ready to test them again. Go through all three checks again. If the vibration is still too great, you might try moving the metal faceplate again. If that doesn't work, not all is lost.

If excessive vibration is still a problem, you may have to cut the rings round again. This time, since you have all the rings glued up in the hollow bowl shape, you'll be cutting them all at once. You will need a band saw for this.

Figure 1-68. Drawing a circle on the plywood faceplate.

Draw a line (circle) on the plywood faceplate by setting up the tool rest on the head stock side of the glued up rings. Draw the line on the plywood faceplate by holding a pencil steady on the tool rest and spin the lathe by hand to draw the circle.

Figure 1-69. Recutting the rings into a new circle in order to help solve the vibration problem.

Once this new circle is drawn, remove the rings from the lathe and cut the rings on the band saw. This will help, but you will still have some vibration. This is because recutting the rings on the band saw only re-centers the outside of the rings. The inside will still be off center. **Mini lathe** users may have to clamp your lathe to a solid (heavy) bench to dampen some of this vibration. Or you might make a bracket to attach to a wall and clamp your lathe to the bracket. This would be an extreme solution, but it should work for the initial turning of the rings. When both the outside and inside of the rings have been turned round, you'll notice the vibration will disappear altogether.

Once you have solved the problem of excessive vibration, it is time to turn the rings into a perfect circle. You may be tempted to turn at a low RPM to reduce vibration. While this would seem to be a good idea, turning too slowly has a tendency to allow the lathe tool to "catch"

Figure 1-70. Turning the rings round.

in the wood. This will place a greater strain on the paper glue joint between the plywood faceplate and the top trim ring. Obviously we do not want this paper glue joint to fail while we are still turning the bowl. Turn the rings at around 1800 RPM when starting out. As the bowl is turned into a perfect circle, both inside and out, you'll be able to turn at an even higher RPM. On final cuts turning at 2800 to 3000 RPM is typical.

(Pay Attention!) Remember back when you made your design ring that you marked the location of the three wooden dowels; now is the time to use this information before you lose track of where they are located. When you cut the design ring into the 9-1/2" circle you may have exposed all three dowels so you already know where the dowels are located. In that case, you're done. However, if they are not visible on the outside surface of the design ring, you must transfer the markings from the design ring to the edge of the plywood faceplate. It is obvious that the markings on the design ring will be turned off immediately, but will remain on the edge of the plywood faceplate, which will not be turned. If all else fails, remember you marked the dowel location on the inside of the design rings as well. You will be able to keep track of their location and remark the outside if necessary. Of course, this only works before you start turning the inside of the bowl.

Figure 1-71. The two arrows point to a dowel appearing in the surface as the rings are turned round.

As you turn the outside of the rings into a perfect circle, you will see the dowels appear and then disappear as you turn deeper into the rings. Be sure to turn away enough material from the outside perimeter of the bowl to completely expose and then turn away all three dowels.

You will also notice that the design (especially the trim rings) appears to "wiggle" up and down. These trim rings do. Due to the accumulated error of drum sanding the rings, and the fact that the surfaces of the plywood faceplate may not be parallel, the trim rings may wiggle. Not to worry, since no one can see all 360 degrees of a

completed bowl at any one time and the bowl will not be spinning as they look at it, they will not be able to see this slight variation in the height of the design and trim rings.

Once the outside is perfectly round and smooth, and all three dowels have disappeared, start turning the inside diameter of the bottom ring perfectly round. **(Pay Attention!)** If your rings were way off center, it may be necessary to turn on the inside of your bowl before completing the outside. In fact, you may have to skip back and forth until both the inside and outside are close to perfectly round. This will reduce the vibration while turning.

Figure 1-72. Turning the inside of the bottom ring on a reversible lathe.

Leave the bottom ring as wide as possible because you will need the extra width when you cut the rabbet joint into this ring. Note that the lathe being used is reversible, so I'm standing on the same side of the lathe at all times. If your lathe is not reversible, simply pull the lathe out from the wall and stand on the other side. Of course you'll have to re-position the tool rest to the opposite side of the bowl when turning from the opposite side of the lathe. **(Pay Attention!)** When you are turning in the reversible mode be sure the faceplate has been tightened well. There is always a danger of catching your lathe tool and having the bowl screw itself off the lathe. Most metal faceplates have a set screw you can tighten to prevent this from happening.

Begin cutting away the inside of the rings until the inside surface of the rings is also smooth and round. Stop and check often to clear shavings and to see if you have turned away enough wood so all inside corners of the butt joints between segments have been cut away. Also

Figure 1-73. Turning the inside of the rings.

check the wall thickness of the rings. You should still have a wall thickness of about 1/2" or more. **Mini lathe** users will find the tool rest that came with your lathe may be too short to allow you to turn all the way into the bowl. I recommend that you purchase an extended tool rest to solve this problem.

Figure 1-74. Turning the final shape of the bowl.

Now it is time to turn the shape of the outside of the bowl. Of course, you had a general shape in your mind when you started out by drawing the profile. At this point start trying to duplicate your original profile drawing. It's not a big deal if your bowl does not perfectly match your original profile drawing. Sometimes wall thickness or a defect in the wood will dictate the bowl's final shape. Or, you may simply just change your mind.

Figure 1-75. Checking the wall thickness.

Once you are satisfied with the final shape of the outside of the bowl, turn the inside shape to match.

Continue turning the inside of the bowl until the thickness approaches 1/4" to 3/8". Bowls with a wall thickness of more than 3/8" are not pleasing to the eye or touch. The wall at the top of the bowl, where it is glued to the faceplate, should be left a little thicker. You'll turn the lip and top few rings to their final shape and thickness after the bottom is glued into the rabbet joint.

As you approach the final shape, both inside and out, take very small final cuts with a very sharp tool. Pay close attention to the bottom few rings (the ones toward the open end of the bowl) as the cut will tend to chatter, especially on the inside. The chattering will occur because you have less stability and more vibration when you're turning farther away from the plywood faceplate.

Figure 1-76. Cutting the rabbet joint with a parting tool.

It is now time to begin cutting the rabbet. Using a parting tool, cut into the bottom ring at a right angle to the ring to a depth of about 3/8". This first cut should be at least 1/2" from the inside edge of the bottom ring. In other words, you want the finished rabbet joint to be at least 1/2" wide, 5/8" would be better. Now make a series of cuts (moving toward the inside edge of the bottom ring) right next to each other until you have completed the full width of the rabbet joint. Smooth the bottom of the rabbet joint you have cut.

Figure 1-77. Checking the rabbet for a flat bottom.

Using a straight edge, check the bottom of the rabbet joint to make sure it is flat and in the same plane. Since this will be a glue joint, it is crucial to have a flat surface at the bottom of the rabbet.

Once the rabbet joint is complete you need to sand the inside edge of the bottom ring. **(Pay Attention!)** Do not sand any portion of the rabbet joint you have cut into the bottom ring. Only sand the inside edge of the bottom ring where it meets the rabbet. Sanding the rabbet joint will change its shape. We want the rabbet joint to be clean, straight, and at a 90 degree angle. As you will see later, you will turn and sand the bottom of the bowl separately. We will do this with the intention of **never** touching the bottom again. We sand the inside of this bottom ring now because it is very difficult to sand the inside of the bowl and not touch the bottom with abrasive paper.

Since we are on the subject of sanding, let's discuss abrasive paper. I use nothing but "A" weight garnet abrasive paper: "A" weight paper is more flexible and follows the contours of the curved surfaces of bowls better than heavier weight papers. I believe that garnet abrasive stays sharper longer (not everyone agrees with this assessment). I start with 80 grit and progress to 100, 150, 220, and finally 280 grit. I'm satisfied with this type of abrasive paper and progression. If you have a different philosophy of abrasive paper, use yours instead. In any case, make sure the inside of the bottom ring is sanded now.

(Pay Attention!) Raise your hand if you like to sand! The most important step in finishing any wood working project is proper preparation. Yes, I mean sanding! No matter how well it is made, a project will be judged by its finish. Scratches left from sanding show poor craftsmanship. Most of the time, scratches left from sanding are because the wood worker has skipped through the grits too fast or has skipped an entire grit. Be sure you have thoroughly sanded with each grit before moving on to the next.

When you're satisfied with both shape and wall thickness of the rings and you have inspected the surfaces for defects, you may remove your turning from the lathe. It is time to remove the metal faceplate. **(Pay Attention!)** Before you remove the metal faceplate, make sure everything is the way you want it. Once you remove the metal faceplate, you cannot go back. You will never be able

Figure 1-78. Using a sharp chisel and mallet to remove the plywood faceplate.

get the bowl back on center (even when you think you're using the same screw holes) to touch up something later.

Next remove the plywood faceplate, which is easy. I do this by sitting on a stool with the bowl in my lap. Using a sharp, wide chisel and a mallet, place the edge of the chisel on the glue line between the top trim ring and the plywood faceplate. Then, tap on the handle of the chisel.

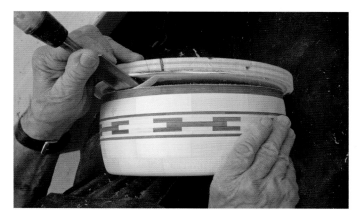

Figure 1-79. Removing the plywood faceplate.

After a few taps, the bowl and plywood faceplate will part. The paper will tear in half. Half remains on the plywood faceplate and half on the top trim ring. That's all there is to it.

Measure the inside diameter of the rabbet joint that you turned into the bottom ring. Use a band saw to cut your Eastern Maple bottom into a circle at a diameter approximately 1/2" larger than the measured diameter of the rabbet joint. Using screws, mount the metal faceplate on the plywood faceplate in the exact center. Again, making sure the screws do not go all the way through the plywood. In this case, if the screws were to pierce the plywood faceplate they would mar the bottom of the bowl. Mount the bottom of the bowl on the lathe. Remember, if you are a **mini lathe** user with a smaller faceplate, double the thickness of the plywood faceplate so you can use longer screws.

Mount the bottom on the lathe and turn it round. Continue turning the bottom until it "just fits" into the rabbet joint you turned into the bottom ring of the bowl. This must be very precise. As the bottom is turned close

Figure 1-80. Sanding the outside diameter of the bottom until it just fits into the rabbet joint turned on the rings.

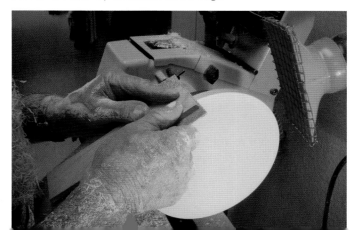

to the exact diameter of the rabbet joint, **GO SLOWLY!** It's a process of making small cuts and frequently checking the bottom to see if it fits the rabbet joint. Repeat this process several times until you achieve a "slip" fit (not a "friction fit") of the bottom into the rabbet joint. I usually "sand" rather than cut, towards the end of this operation. In other words, I "creep" up on the final diameter slowly. A sloppy joint looks bad and allows the bowl to be off center during the final turning.

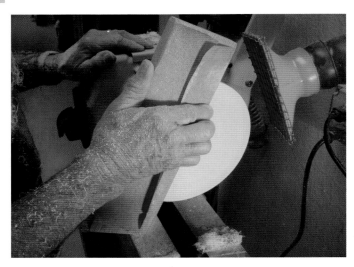

Figure 1-83. Sanding the "flat" with a wood block and abrasive paper.

Figure 1-81. Checking the bottom for a "slip" fit into the rabbet joint cut into the bottom rings.

Once the bottom fits the rabbet joint, face the bottom (turn it perfectly flat) with the same scraper tool you used for turning the rings.

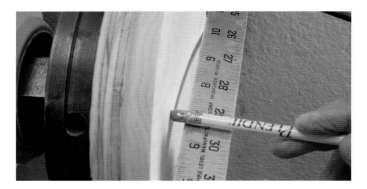

Figure 1-82. Using a straight edge and pencil to check for the amount of "dish."

Next, turn a "dish" into the bottom. The center of the dished bottom should be approximately 3/8" thick. You must also leave a flat surface around the perimeter approximately 3/4" wide.

This 3/4" "flat" is for completing the rabbet joint. Obviously, you want a flat area around the perimeter of the bottom to fit into the rabbet. Sand this 3/4" "flat" with abrasive paper wrapped around a wood block. Use a low RPM on the lathe to avoid burning the abrasive paper.

Once the "dish" is turned, start sanding the bottom. Sand with each grit up through 220 on the bottom of the bowl. The idea is to **NEVER** touch the bottom again with anything but 280 grit abrasive paper on the final sanding of the bowl. It is very difficult to do any turning or heavy

sanding of the bottom once it is glued into the rings. So, make sure you're satisfied with the bottom before gluing it into the rings. Remember, you are sanding "across" grain half the time when sanding the bottom, Because of this, I stop the lathe and sand "with" the grain before moving on to the next grit. Circular scratches in the bottom of your bowl will look bad!

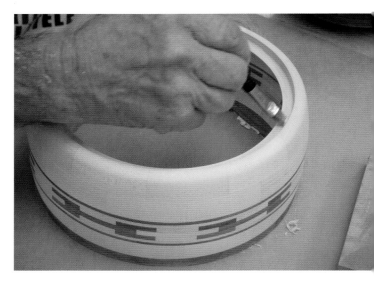

Figure 1-84. Carefully apply glue with a good glue brush.

With the sanding of the bottom complete, remove the turned bottom from the lathe, but **(Pay Attention!)** do not remove the metal faceplate at this time. Now glue it into the rabbet joint. No sloppy gluing on this procedure. Glue "squeeze out" is a no-no! Apply glue with a small, stiff artist brush being careful not to get glue on anything but the glue joint. Take your time!

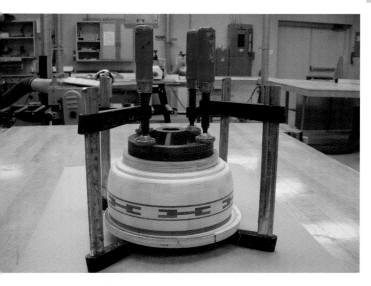

Figure 1-85. Gluing the bottom into the turned rings.

Use at least four clamps with a plywood glue block on the top trim ring. Set aside this glued-up bowl overnight to allow the glue to cure.

Figure 1-86. The bowl is now ready to be turned into its final shape. Note that half of the paper from the glue joint is still in place.

Once the glue is cured, mount the bowl back on the lathe. This time, of course, the bottom will be mounted to the head stock and the top trim ring will be closest to you. This top ring will still have the paper left over from the glue joint.

Finish turning the lip and any other areas that need to be turned down to the final thickness. Do not touch the finished and sanded bottom unless there is a defect that cannot be ignored. Using a low RPM to avoid burning, sand both the inside and out with the 80 grit progressing through to 280 grit sequence. The bottom, of course, is not to be touched with any abrasive paper until you reach the 280 grit. At that point, sand the entire bowl, inside and out, with 280 grit. Of course, all of this sanding can be done right on the lathe.

With the finish sanding complete, remove the bowl from the lathe and take off the metal faceplate. Remove the plywood faceplate with the chisel and mallet as you did before when removing the plywood faceplate from the rings.

Figure 1-87. This padded fixture is designed to hold the bowl while scraping off the paper and glue.

Now you have the problem of removing the paper from the bottom of the bowl. Sanding the paper off is an option and with enough sanding you will be able to remove it. However, I use a #80 cabinet scraper. I have made a

Figure 1-88. Using a cabinet scraper to remove paper and glue from the bottom.

fixture to hold the bowl while I use the scraper to remove the paper and glue from the bottom.

Using a cabinet scraper is much faster than sanding off the paper and glue. Plus it is more accurate for keeping the bottom flat. **(Pay Attention!)** I know you will be tempted to use some sort of a powered belt or disc sander for removing the paper and glue. While it can be done, it is also the fastest way to ruin all of your hard work. It is very difficult to accurately sand the bottom flat with these power sanders. After scraping, sand the bottom with each of the abrasive grits used on the final sanding of the bowl.

Since this is intended to be a salad bowl, I recommend that you use Salad Bowl Finish™ made by General Finishes. It is easy to apply and gives a gloss finish. You simply apply it with a piece of old T-shirt. Start by applying at least three coats to the bottom of the bowl. Sand between coats with 400 grit wet and dry abrasive paper. Set the bowl on its finished bottom and apply at least three coats to the inside and outside of the bowl. I generally apply four coats when I finish a salad bowl. However, you may have your own favorite technique for finishing your projects. Use the technique that you are most comfortable with.

Figure 1-89. Finished salad bowl.

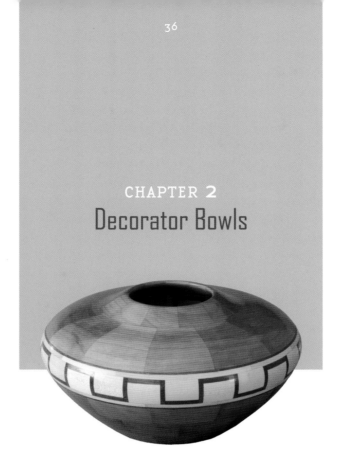

CHAPTER 2
Decorator Bowls

2-1:
Planning the Decorator Bowl

I consider a decorator bowl to be one with a closed top and a small diameter opening. These bowls are turned in two halves and joined together somewhere around the middle. They do not really have a utilitarian value except for their beauty. They are fun to make and worth the challenge.

The basic techniques used in making the "L" shaped bowls will also apply when making decorator bowls. The major difference is that each ring will be a different diameter. Therefore, even though the segments within each ring will be the same length, there will be a different segment length for each ring. The width of each ring will likely be different as well. As I do when making an "L" shaped bowl, I first draw the profile of the decorator bowl I intend to make.

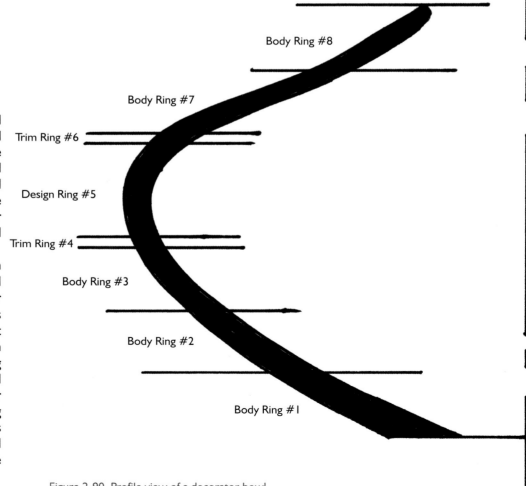

Figure 2-90. Profile view of a decorator bowl.

segments for this design. So let's get started on the design rings. First you will need to laminate up a piece of 3/16" thick Purple Heart to a piece of 3/4" thick Eastern Maple. Both pieces need to be about 1-1/4" wide and 30" long. After the glue has cured, square this lamination before cutting the segments.

Remember, you must cut these segments at half the length of the segments of a 12 segment ring. In this case, it would normally be 1-5/16" long. **(Pay Attention!)** To make a Greek Key design, you must cut it even shorter to accommodate the vertical piece of Purple Heart you will glue in between each segment. These vertical pieces will be 1/8" thick. Therefore, cut your segments at 1-3/16" long. In other words, 1/8" short of the 1-5/16" that would normally be required.

Machine enough Purple Heart to make 24 vertical pieces that will be 1/8" thick by 1-1/4" wide with the length equal to the thickness of the design lamination. These pieces will be glued in between the segments. You will notice in the lamination you made that the Purple Heart layer is thicker than 1/8". However, after you glue up your rings and sand them smooth in the thickness sander, they will match the 1/8" thick vertical pieces.

Figure 2-102. Sets of eight will be glued to the sets of four to make half rings of twelve.

Figure 2-101. Glue up the segments with the vertical pieces in between.

Glue up the segments in pairs with the vertical pieces in between and with every other segment flipped over. Make sure the grain of the 1/8" thick spacers is vertical. This is to avoid end grain turning. Continue gluing up as usual by gluing up pairs into sets of four. Then glue up the sets of four into sets of eight.

Remember to hold out a set of four for every set of eight, so you can glue up the sets of twelve.

(Pay Attention!) Edge sand the two half rings before gluing on the vertical Purple Heart pieces. Then, once they fit, glue the half rings together with the vertical pieces in place. If you were to edge sand them with the vertical pieces in place, they would be too narrow and would not match the other vertical pieces in thickness.

After the glue is cured, run the full rings through the thickness sander. Make sure you sand just enough off each side to bring down the top and bottom layers of Purple Heart to match the thickness of the vertical pieces. At this point I usually glue the spacer (if required) and trim rings to the design ring. The design ring and the two spacer rings (required for this design) should measure about

Figure 2-103. Half rings glued up into a full ring.

1-1/8" thick. The bottom trim ring will add about 1/8". Remember, the top trim ring will be about 3/8" to allow for the rabbet joint.

Cut and glue up the body rings as you did when making the salad bowl. Run each ring through the thickness drum sander to prepare them for gluing. **(Pay Attention!)** Remember the "wiggle" of the trim rings I mentioned when you were turning the salad bowl? The drum thickness may not be adjusted perfectly. It may not be sanding each ring to perfectly parallel faces. This is the reason for the "wiggle" in the trim rings. To solve this problem, once the faces are smooth enough to glue together, run each ring through the sander at least three times **at the same setting.** Turn the ring about 90 degrees each time you run the ring through these last three times. This should solve most of the "wiggle" problem. Since you are trying to match the thickness (at least in appearance) of the bottom trim ring while you are cutting the rabbet in the top trim ring, this "wiggle" problem needs to be solved. I even use this same technique to run the plywood faceplates through the thickness sander to assure parallel faces.

2-3:
Gluing Rings for a
Decorator Bowl

With the salad bowl you glued up all the rings at once. You lined them up in their proper alignment by eye. Gluing up the rings for the decorator bowl will be different. First, you will glue up rings in sub-assemblies of two rings at a time. Plus you will need to be more precise in their alignment. So let's get started.

Figure 2-104. Drawing a circle on the glued up ring of Cherry.

First you need to be more precise in cutting the rings into perfect circles. Carefully draw a circle that just fits inside the edges of the ring. Cut it out on the band saw. I recommend you then edge sand the rings to the circle you just drew. You need to complete this step for each ring.

You will glue the bowl up in sub-assemblies. Gluing ring #1 to ring #2 will form the first sub-assembly. Then adding ring #3 to the sub-assembly of rings #1 and #2. Each step must be as accurate as possible to keep the entire bowl on center.

First, you will need to locate the exact position that ring #1 will be glued to ring #2. Use double-sided tape to attach a block of wood to the bench. Set your compass

Figure 2-105. Centering ring #2 to establish the gluing location of ring #1.

to the radius of the ring. With the compass point on the block, move the ring into a position so the pencil point will touch the line you drew to cut the ring into a circle. Check in several places around the circle to be sure ring #2 is centered.

Being careful to not move ring #2 out of position, set your compass to slightly larger than the radius of ring #1 and draw a circle on ring #2. Check to make sure ring #1 fits inside of this circle. Remember to align the rings into the brick wall configuration. Place index marks in at least three places around the perimeter of ring #1.

Figure 2-106. Drawing a circle on ring #2 to establish the gluing location for ring #1.

Figure 2-107. Gluing ring #1 to ring #2. Note the index marks to make sure you can check for movement during the clamping process.

Apply glue to both rings. Using glue blocks, top and bottom, clamp this sub-assembly together. The index marks will indicate if the rings start to slip during the clamping process. It's important that the alignment and centering be as perfect as possible. There will be less room for error when turning a decorator bowl compared to the salad bowl.

Continue the same process of using a compass to center the rings with each other.

The order of gluing the bottom half of the bowl will be:

Glue rings #1 and #2 to ring #3.
Glue rings #1, #2, and #3 to the Design Ring (assuming the spacer and trim rings have already been glued to the design ring).
Glue the sub-assembly of rings #1,# 2, #3, and the design rings to a plywood faceplate with paper in between.

The order of gluing for the top half of the bowl will be:

Glue ring #8 to ring #7.
Glue sub-assembly of rings #7 and #8 to a waste block **with no paper in between.**

Notice two points in the gluing process. First, a plywood faceplate will be glued to the design ring with paper in between for easy removal. The bottom half will be turned "upside down" like the salad bowl. A rabbet joint will be turned into ring #1 to accept a bottom, also just like the salad bowl. Second, the waste block glued to the top half of the bowl (ring #8) will not have paper glued in between. Although I have always had excellent success in using a paper glue joint, the smaller surface area of this glue joint makes me a little nervous. Having to saw off the waste piece is a small price to pay for peace of mind.

Obviously, you will be attaching a metal faceplate to both the top and bottom of the bowl. This will allow you to turn each half separately.

Remember, **mini lathe** users may have to double the thickness of the plywood faceplate and waste block to accommodate longer screws.

2-4:
Turning the Decorator Bowl

Once the top and bottom halves of the decorator bowl have been glued up, it is time to turn each half. Start by turning the bottom half first.

Figure 2-108. The bottom half of the bowl is ready to be turned to its intended shape. Note the index marks that were used for alignment during gluing.

Attach the metal faceplate to the plywood faceplate. Mount the bowl on the lathe and make the same vibration tests as you did for the salad bowl. Hopefully your gluing was accurate enough to be able to turn the bowl as is. If not, adjust as necessary.

After solving any problems you may have with vibration, turn the lower portion of the bowl to its intended shape. Notice in Figure 2-108 that the top trim ring is much thicker than the bottom trim ring. Remember, a rabbet joint will be cut into this trim ring. During that process, the top trim ring will be turned to appear to match the thickness of the bottom trim ring.

Figure 2-109. Lower half of the bowl turned to its basic shape. Arrow indicates the thicker top trim ring for the rabbet joint.

Figure 2-110. Rabbet joint has been turned into the bottom of the bowl.

Turn a rabbet joint into the bottom of the bowl. Make sure it is flat and at a 90 degree angle for the best glue joint. Glue a waste piece of wood to a piece of Cherry that is larger than the diameter of the rabbet joint. This will be turned to fit the rabbet joint in the bottom ring. Again, because of the small surface area, I would recommend not using paper in between. Turn the bottom with the same techniques that you employed when turning the salad bowl

bottom. I often turn the bottom of a decorator bowl flush with the bottom ring rather than leaving a foot.

After the bottom has been glued into the bowl, mount it on the lathe and turn the inside to shape. Turn the wall thickness down to 3/8" or less. Thicker walls equate to a heavy bowl. Part of the aesthetics of a turned bowl will be in its feel and weight. Bowls that feel too heavy are not as pleasing.

Figure 2-111. The inside of the bowl has been turned to shape. Note the rabbet joint turned into the top trim ring.

Turn a rabbet joint into the outside edge of the top trim ring. This joint is designed to fit the top and bottom halves of the bowl together accurately. Also, by cutting the rabbet joint into the outside edge of the top trim ring, it will start to appear to match the bottom trim ring in thickness.

Figure 2-112. The top half of the bowl has been turned to its intended shape. Note the rabbet joint turned on the inside edge of ring #7.

Check the depth of the rabbet joint frequently. As you are turning the rabbet joint you are attempting to cut away just enough of the outside edge of ring #6 so it will be the same thickness as ring #4. Leave the wall thickness in the area of the rabbet joint a little heavy. This will be turned away as you fit the two rabbets together. Sand the inside of the bottom half going through all the grits.

Mount the top half of the bowl and check for excessive vibration—adjust as necessary. Turn it into its intended shape, both inside and out. Check both the inside and outside diameter frequently as you want to match the bottom half. Turn a rabbet in the inside edge to fit the rabbet in the bottom half. **Go slowly!** You want the two halves to "slip fit" together with no slop.

Turning the inside in the lip area is a little tricky. Because it is attached to a waste piece, you cannot turn the outside of the lip to its final shape. You have to visualize the shape that the outside will be after it is turned. You must turn the inside to match what you think the outside will look like. Sand the inside of the top half of the bowl.

Figure 2-113. Using the tail stock spindle to clamp the two halves together when gluing.

After the insides of both the top and bottom have been sanded, you should make a final check of the "fit" of the rabbet joint. **(Pay Attention!)** Make this check before removing the metal faceplate from the top half of the bowl. With both metal faceplates still attached, you can still touch up the rabbet joint on either the top or bottom if some adjustment is required. When you are satisfied with the fit of the rabbet joint, remove the metal faceplate (but not the waste block) from the top half of the bowl. You're not finished turning yet, so the faceplate on the bottom must remain in place. Apply small amounts of glue to the surfaces of both sides of the rabbet joints. Place the top in position, remembering to line up the brick wall alignment. You may want to use index marks to avoid misalignment. Hold the top in place while moving the tail stock close enough to use

it for clamping. Crank the spindle against the waste stock faceplate to apply clamping pressure. **(Pay Attention!)** The threads of the tail stock are very powerful. Do not apply too much pressure. It is possible to crack the thin walls of your bowl or break one of the butt joints between the segments with too much pressure.

Figure 2-114. The live center in the tail stock will support the bowl for final turning and sanding.

Allow the glue to cure. Install a cup center or a live center into the tail stock and crank the spindle up against the wood waste block. This will support the bowl while completing the final turning and sanding of the glued up bowl. There will always be a need to turn the area at the rabbet joint. Carefully turn this area to smooth up the joint and finish the curve of the bowl. Sand the entire bowl with

Figure 2-115. With the faceplate removed, turn the lip to its final shape.

all of the grits. Of course you will still have to turn and sand the lip, but sand most of the bowl now. With most of the sanding finished, use a parting tool to cut off the top waste block as far as you dare. Back off the tail stock and finish cutting away the waste block with a hand saw.

After removing the waste block, carefully turn and sand the lip to its final shape. Now do you see why we did not use paper when gluing the waste block to the bottom of the bowl? The lip should be less than 1/4" thick when finished.

Using the same procedure, remove the bottom waste block with a parting tool and hand saw. **(Pay Attention!)** The screws used to attach the metal faceplate to the waste block may be too long to do this on the lathe. You may have to remove the metal faceplate and saw off the wood waste block after removing the bowl from the lathe.

Either sand or scrape the small amount of wood left from the waste block. Complete the bowl by sanding the bottom with each grit up through 280. Apply the finish of your choice.

I usually finish the inside of a decorator bowl with a paste varnish like General Finishes' Gel Topcoat™. It is very difficult to obtain a smooth finish on the inside of a bowl with a small opening. Using a paste varnish allows you to wipe it on and wipe it off. You can also apply the same paste varnish to the outside of the bowl if you desire a satin finish. To obtain a gloss finish, I usually use a product by General Finishes called Arm-R-Seal™. Like the Salad Bowl Finish™, you apply it with a piece of old T-shirt. Of course, you may have your own technique for finishing. Use whatever technique makes you comfortable.

Figure 2-116. Finished decorator bowl.

CHAPTER 3
Serving Platters

3-1: Planning a Serving Platter

Making a serving platter with a segmented ring around the edge is just an extension of making a segmented bowl. The twist is, the design is incorporated in the bottom of the platter as opposed to the body of the bowl. While I use a total of three rings around the perimeter of the platter, they are very thin. The total height of a typical finished platter is seldom more than 1-1/4". The diameter, of course, will be determined by the swing of your lathe.

While I normally do not make a profile drawing of a platter, I have drawn one for the purpose of this book. As you can see in Figure 3-117, the three rings are all the same diameter and are quite thin. The bottom ring will be about 1/2" thick. The bottom ring is also wider than the other two to accommodate the rabbet joint for the bottom. The middle ring is about 1/8" thick and the top trim ring is about 1/4" thick. The top and bottom rings will have 12 segments each. The middle ring will have 24 segments.

Start by using your geometry skills to determine the length of the segments. Like the salad bowl, all three rings will be the same diameter so you only need to make one drawing to determine their length. Since I use a lathe that has a 16" swing, I will be describing how to make a platter with a diameter of about 15-1/2". The steps are the same for a platter of any diameter.

Segmented Rings

Figure 3-117. Profile view of a serving platter.

Let's review the steps:

Draw a circle at the desired diameter.
Mark off one radius on the perimeter of the circle.
Draw a line through the center
   and the two radii marks.
Bisect the resulting angle to obtain 1/12 of the circle.
Measure out along two adjacent lines about 1/2".
Connect the marks with a straight line.
The measured length of this line is the length
   of the segments for all three rings.

It turns out that the measured length of a segment for a 15-1/2" diameter bowl is 4-1/8". If you have forgotten how to do one or more of the steps, go back to the description of these steps in Chapter 1-1 of this book.

3-2:
Turning the
Rings for a Platter

Always make the rings first, as you would when making a bowl. The rabbet turned into the rings will determine the size of the bottom and therefore the size of the design required for the platter. Let's list the segments we will need for this platter.

	THICKNESS	WIDTH	LENGTH	
Top ring	1/4"	1-1/4"	4-1/8"	12 segments
Middle ring	1/8"	1-1/4"	2-1/16"	24 segments
Bottom ring	1/2"	1-1/2"	4-1/8"	12 segments

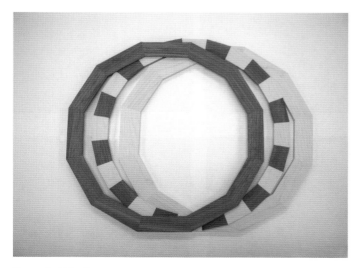

Figure 3-118. Platter rings from left to right: trim ring, middle ring, and bottom ring.

Machine out the material you'll need for your platter. You can use the dimensions in the above list if you are using a lathe with a 16" swing. Smaller lathes will, of course, require segments of a different length. Cut your segments to the length required for your platter.

Friction glue the segments together into the required rings. As you can see, I have decided to make the middle ring with Eastern Maple and Padauk. The top trim ring is Padauk and the bottom ring is Eastern Maple. You, of course, may use any type of wood you wish. When the glue has cured, sand the rings smooth in the thickness drum sander.

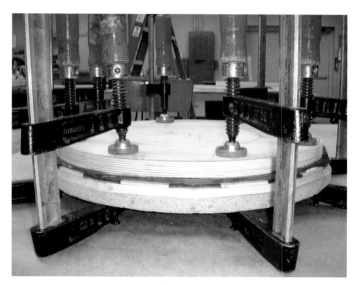

Figure 3-119. Glue up platter rings with plywood faceplate in place. Note the bottom press board disc is a glue block and is not glued to the bottom ring.

Glue your rings together in the same brick wall configuration as usual. A plywood faceplate needs to be glued to the top trim ring. Remember to glue paper in between. On larger diameter platters or bowls I use a good quality plywood for the faceplate, usually Baltic Birch. **Mini lathe** users may want to double the thickness of the plywood faceplate to accommodate longer screws. There is no need to "pin" these rings together before gluing. In fact, I don't even cut the rings into a circle before gluing them up.

Install a metal faceplate on the plywood faceplate. Mount the rings on the lathe and adjust the tool rest so you can draw a circle on the top trim ring. Cut this circle on the band saw before you start turning the rings. You can skip this step if you don't mind turning off the corners of the segments. This set of rings is very easy to turn. As usual, check for excessive vibration before starting to turn the rings.

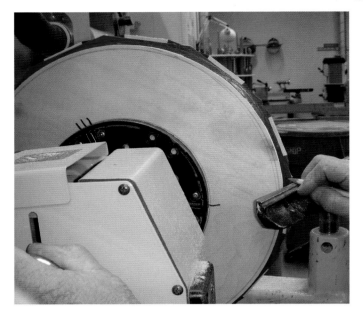

Figure 3-120. Drawing the circle on the bottom ring of the glued up rings.

Figure 3-121. Checking the "flatness" of the rabbet with a straight edge.

As you did with the salad and decorator bowls, turn the rings into a perfect circle. Turn a pleasing curve on the bottom ring. Also turn a rabbet into the bottom ring. This rabbet should be just over 1/4" deep and at least 1/2" wide. Check that you have turned a flat bottom on the rabbet with 90 degree sides.

When you're totally satisfied with the rabbet and shape of the rings, remove them from the lathe and take off the metal faceplate. Remove the plywood faceplate with a chisel and mallet and set the rings aside.

3-3: Planning the Primary Design

The focal point of the platter is the design in the bottom. Most of the designs I use are influenced by the Native American culture of the Southwest. Of course, you may use any design you choose. I normally place a primary design in the center of the bottom, along with two secondary designs, one on each side of the primary design. Appendix B has several examples for both primary and secondary designs that could be used in platters. The possibilities for other designs is only limited by your imagination.

I always machine out strips of wood 2" wide for these designs. After the designs are glued up, I re-saw them. By re-sawing, I get two designs out of one. Each design will be about 7/8" thick. I end up with an extra primary design, but once you start making platters it will be hard to quit. You will soon put the extra primary design in the next platter. Obviously the two primary designs will be identical. But, by using a different secondary design, you'll have two different platters.

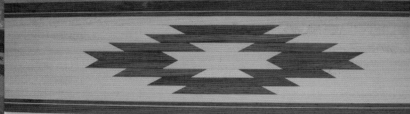

Figure 3-122. Example of a star burst primary design.

Frequently I start off with a "starburst" as my primary design, as shown in Figure 3-122. While it may look complicated, it really isn't that difficult to make. I always make a full size drawing of both the primary and secondary designs so I can establish the exact size of each piece. I then make a cutting list that includes the number and size of each piece. Both the primary and secondary designs will require "pinning" to keep the design pieces in line while gluing. Therefore, I make the designs extra-long to allow space for the wood dowel.

You will notice that the spacer pieces are 17" long in the drawing in Figure 3-123. To determine the length of the design required for your platter, measure the inside diameter of the rabbet in the segmented ring. Add about three inches for the dowels. In the platter I'm describing, the inside dimension was 14". Therefore, I'm making the primary and secondary designs 17" long. The dimensions listed on the filler pieces to the left and right of the design will also be long enough for the desired 17" length.

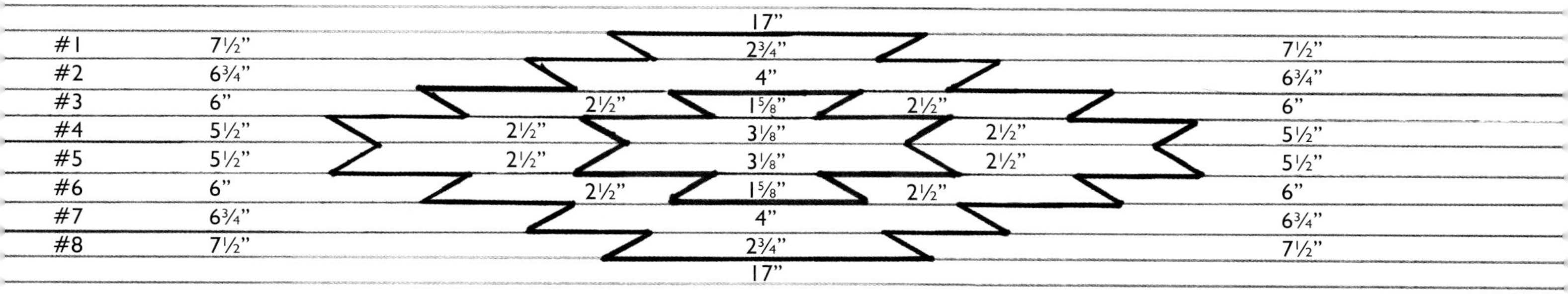

			17"				
#1	7½"		2¾"			7½"	
#2	6¾"		4"			6¾"	
#3	6"	2½"	1⅝"	2½"		6"	
#4	5½"	2½"	3⅛"	2½"		5½"	
#5	5½"	2½"	3⅛"	2½"		5½"	
#6	6"	2½"	1⅝"	2½"		6"	
#7	6¾"		4"			6¾"	
#8	7½"		2¾"			7½"	
			17"				

Figure 3-123. Drawing of the star burst design. Note the length of each piece is listed.

The spacer and trim pieces (above and below the design) are all 2" wide and 17" long, only their thickness will vary. Therefore, let's use the drawing in Figure 3-123 to make a cutting list for the design, filler, spacer, and trim pieces by layer and type of wood. Let's start with the design first.

	THICKNESS	WIDTH	LENGTH
Padauk design pieces:			
Layers #1 & #8 two at	5/16"	2"	2-3/4"
Layers #2 & #7 two at	5/16"	2"	4"
Layers #3 & #6 four at	5/16"	2"	2-1/2"
Layers #4 & #5 four at	5/16"	2"	2-1/2"
Eastern Maple design pieces in middle of starburst:			
Layers #3 & #6 two at	5/16"	2"	1-5/8"
Layers #4 & #5 two at	5/16"	2"	3-1/8"
Eastern Maple filler pieces to the right and left of design:			
Layers #1 & #8 four at	5/16"	2"	7-1/2"
Layers #2 & #7 four at	5/16"	2"	6-3/4"
Layers #3 & #6 four at	5/16"	2"	6"
Layers #4 & #5 four at	5/16"	2"	5-1/2"
Eastern Maple and Padauk trim pieces:			
Cut as needed for your design. Note that Figure 3-122 shows I used two pieces of Eastern Maple (spacers) and two pieces of Padauk (trim) both above and below the primary design.			

I typically cut all the pieces for the starburst about 1/8" too long. Then when you cut the bevel on the ends, they will be about the right length. The length of the pieces in this design is not critical. It's the relative proportion between pieces that counts. However, the length of the Eastern Maple filler pieces to the right and left of the starburst must be long enough to allow for a dowel at each end. By the way, the starburst design in Figure 3-123 is about 7-1/2" long. This may be too large for a smaller platter. Adjust accordingly for the diameter of your platter.

3-4:
Sixty Degree Fixture

Cutting bevels on the ends of the starburst design present a special problem. This design calls for a 30 degree bevel on the ends. It's easy to cut a 45 degree bevel on the table saw, but not 30 degree bevels. Forty-five degree bevels simply do not have the same "look" as the 30 degree bevel.

Figure 3-124. Using a fixture like the one pictured here allows for cutting a 30 degree bevel with no set-up time.

While there are a number of ways to cut the bevel on the end of the pieces that make up the starburst design, all but one will require set-up time. That one, of course, requires you to build a fixture. But once you build the fixture, you will not have to spend time setting up to make 30 degree bevels. This fixture allows you to leave the blade in its normal position. That is, at a 90 degree angle to the top of the table saw. It's called a 60 degree fixture because the fixture holds the wood at a 60 degree angle to the blade. If the blade is set at its normal 90 degree angle, the resulting cut is 30 degrees.

Figure 3-125. Build a 90 degree sliding cutoff table.

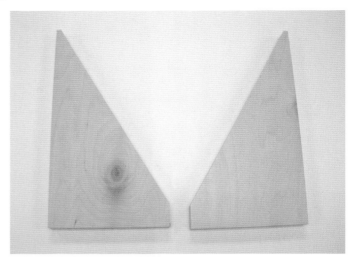

Figure 3-127. Completed triangles.

Start by building a 90 degree sliding cutoff table. The plywood base should be 1/2" thick by about 16" by 24". Make both the primary and secondary fences out of pine. No need for the primary fence to be made out of hardwood. It will not have to function as a chip breaker.

Your triangles should look like the ones in Figure 3-127. Accuracy is the key. Make sure both triangles are exactly the same.

Measure the distance between the primary and secondary fences on your cutoff table. Subtract the thickness of the two triangles. On the cutoff table being used in this example, the measurement was 14-1/2". I subtracted the thickness of my triangles and got 13-1/16". Machine out a piece of 3/4" plywood 10" wide and to the length required for your cutoff table. This is the bevel plate and will hold your wood at the correct angle when cutting the bevels.

Figure 3-126. Trim about 1/2" off the points of a 60 degree plywood triangles.

Next you'll make a bevel plate assembly to install in the sliding cutoff table. This will hold your wood at a 60 degree angle to the top of the table saw. Machine out two 30/60/90 degree triangles from 3/4" plywood or pine. Make the longest edge about 10" long. Trim off about 1/2" from the 60 degree points. **(Pay Attention!)** Cut off the points accurately. Both at the same time, as shown in Figure 3-126. This "flat" on the points of the triangles will be used later to line up the bevel plate with the saw kerf in the plywood base.

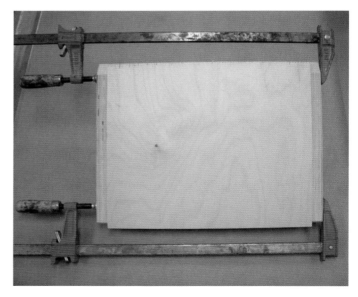

Figure 3-128. Bevel plate with both triangles clamped in place.

Carefully clamp the bevel plate between the two triangles. Make sure the bevel plate is flush with the edge of the triangles. The overall length of this assembly should just fit in between the primary and secondary fences of your sliding cutoff table.

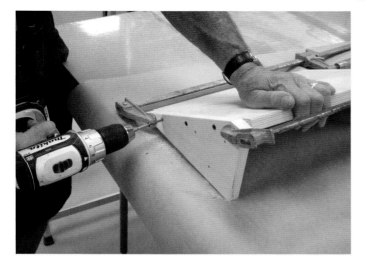

Figure 3-129. Attaching triangles to bevel plate with screws.

Attach the triangles to the bevel plate with screws. Do not use glue. Eventually the fixture will wear out. By not using glue on your fixtures, you can easily take them apart and rebuild them if necessary.

Figure 3-130. Attaching the triangles to the 90 degree sliding cutoff table.

Place the bevel plate assembly with the attached triangles on the sliding cutoff table. Align the "flats" of the triangles to the saw kerf in the sliding cutoff table. Clamp the assembly in place and attach with screws to the two fences. This alignment is important because you want the bevel plate to be parallel to the saw kerf in the cutoff table.

Figure 3-131. The triangle and bevel plate assembly is now in place. Note you can see the saw kerf in the two corners next to the two fences.

Lower the table saw blade and place the sliding cutoff table back on the table saw. Both of the "flats" you cut on the support triangles should be flush with the saw kerf. The bevel plate will extend over the saw kerf as it still needs to be trimmed off to match the flat points of the two triangles.

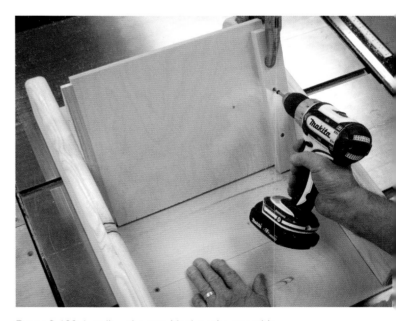

Figure 3-132. Installing the stop block to the assembly.

Before trimming the bevel plate, install a hardwood stop block parallel with the edge of the bevel plate assembly. This stop block will hold the wood at a 90 degree angle to the saw kerf and act as a chip breaker as well.

Figure 3-133. Trimming the bevel plate and stop block.

Raise the blade, turn on the saw, and trim both the bevel plate and the stop block. Now the two triangles, the bevel plate and the stop block will all be in the same plane.

Figure 3-134. A toggle clamp makes cutting the bevels more accurate and safer.

Although you do not need to install a toggle clamp to hold the wood you're cutting, I recommend it. While you can hold long pieces with your hand, holding short pieces can be "very exciting." I also believe you will obtain more accurate cuts when using a clamp. The exact location of the toggle clamp will be up to you. **(Pay Attention!)** If you install the clamp too low, there will be a chance that the saw blade will cut into the clamp. If you install it too high, it will prevent you from cutting the shorter pieces for your design. I recommend that you install the toggle clamp so you can hold and cut pieces that are about 2" long. Note the black horizontal line you see on the bevel plate assembly. This is to remind you that the blade must be at or below this line to prevent cutting into the toggle clamp.

Figure 3-135. Finished 60 degree cut off table.

In Figure 3-135 you'll also notice a second stop block parallel to the saw kerf. I normally install this stop block with double-sided tape. The height of this stop block must be determined by trial and error. The function of this stop block is to keep the wood you're cutting from sliding too far down the bevel plate. You want to cut the least amount off each piece and still cut the desired bevel. Adjust as necessary so you're not wasting wood by cutting off too much.

3-5:
Cutting the Primary Design

Machine out enough stock to make your design pieces. Remember you're making all the pieces 2" wide for re-sawing later. Using your cutting list, cut the pieces for your primary design to length. Remember to cut them about 1/8" too long to allow for cutting the bevel. You will cut these pieces to length in the 90 degree sliding cut off table. The bevels will be cut later.

Figure 3-136. Checking that there are no missing pieces. Note that one end of the 1-5/8" Eastern Maple has already been beveled.

After cutting all the pieces to exact length (plus 1/8") stack them up in order to be sure you have cut all of the required pieces. Notice that the two short Eastern Maple pieces **must** be beveled on one end **before** cutting them to length. This is because they are too short to bevel in your 60 degree fixture. More about cutting these short pieces will follow.

Figure 3-137. Cutting a bevel on a design piece.

All of the pieces in a starburst design will require a 30 degree bevel on at least one end if not both. Bevel the ends of the pieces in your new 60 degree sliding cutoff table on the table saw.

Figure 3-138. These eight Padauk pieces have their bevels cut to form a parallelogram. Note the two pieces of Eastern Maple are already glued to the Padauk pieces.

(Pay Attention!) If you're making the starburst design that requires two contrasting woods, you must keep close track of the direction of the bevels. Note the direction of the bevels on the pieces of Padauk in Figure 3-138. The beveled ends on these pieces form a parallelogram. All of the other pieces are cut into a wedge shape.

When your design requires shorter pieces than you can cut with your 60 degree sliding cutoff table, there is a solution for this. As you can see in Figure 3-138, two of the Padauk pieces are already glued to the shorter Eastern Maple. This is done so you can cut the bevels on these short pieces. In the example I'm using, the design calls for two pieces of Eastern Maple that are 1-5/8" long. Both pieces require bevels on their ends. The 60 degree cutoff table will only cut bevels on pieces that are about 2" or longer. To solve this problem, cut a bevel on the ends of two pieces of Eastern Maple that are longer than 2". Then cut the opposite ends to the required length at a 90 degree angle. In this case, 1-5/8" plus 1/8" for a total length of 1-3/4" long. The adjacent pieces of Padauk are 2-1/2" long.

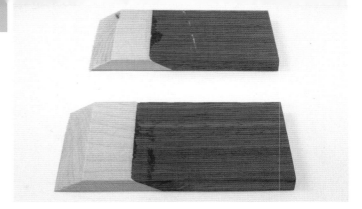

Figure 3-139. Eastern Maple and Padauk glued together to make a total length that exceeds 2". This is more than enough to cut the required bevels.

By gluing the Eastern Maple piece to the Padauk piece, you'll have enough total length to cut the bevel on the other end of the Eastern Maple. The procedure for gluing the bevels together is explained in Chapter 3-6.

Figure 3-140. Cutting the bevel on a piece that is too short to bevel without gluing it to a longer piece.

With the 1-5/8" piece of Eastern Maple glued to the adjacent piece of Padauk, you can now use the toggle clamp to hold it in the 60 degree fixture. This allows you to safely cut the bevel on the other end of the piece of Eastern Maple.

Figure 3-141. Checking that all the pieces have the correct bevels. Note that these pieces are not yet glued together.

With the bevels cut, stack up all the pieces to check that all bevels have been cut correctly. If all the pieces fit, you're ready to glue up your design.

3-6: Gluing Up the Primary Design

Before you glue your design together, check to see if the opposite and matching pieces are the same length, especially pieces in the center of your design. This design is supposed to be symmetrical. Pieces that have somehow been cut to different lengths will not match up. This, of course, spoils the symmetry of the design.

Once you're satisfied with the length of all your design pieces, lay them all out in order. You'll use "friction" gluing to join them together. Apply glue and rub them back and forth as you did when gluing segments together. Make sure you glue them up with their edges in a straight line.

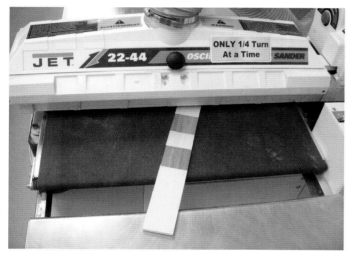

Figure 3-142. Sanding each layer of the design in the drum sander.

After the glue has cured, you'll note that the faces will not be flat enough to glue together at this point. Take them to the drum thickness sander and sand them flat. Sand each side of each layer the same number of times. I find that it generally takes two passes on each side before the faces are smooth enough to glue together.

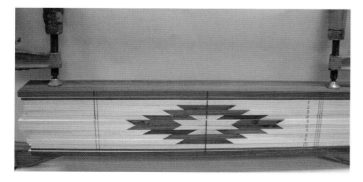

Figure 3-143. Complete design clamped together. Note the reference marks and numbers.

After sanding, mark the center of the design on each layer. Carefully line up the center marks and clamp the layers together. Using a try square, draw some reference lines across the layers. I also number the layers of the design. This helps to keep the layers in order when gluing them up. Also cut top and bottom trim layers and add them to your design.

It is best if you "pin" the design layers before gluing. As usual, when glue is applied, the layers will slip during the gluing process. I generally do not worry about pinning the top and bottom trim layers.

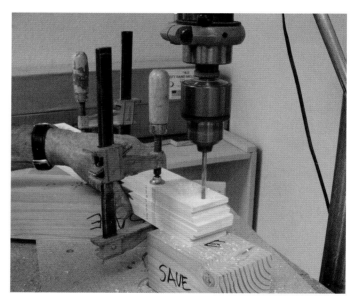

Figure 3-144. Drilling a 13/64" hole for a 3/16" dowel.

Clamp the design layers together and drill two 13/64" holes to accept a 3/16" wood dowel. Drill one hole in each end of the design layers. Remember you made the design layers extra-long to allow space for the dowels. Frequently, as in this case, I am not able to find a drill long enough to drill through the design pieces and the top and bottom spacers as well. Therefore, you will notice I have left out the top and bottom spacer and trim pieces in this drilling operation.

However, at some point, you also must glue at least a spacer piece to the top and bottom of your design layers. (I always glue both a spacer and trim layer to my design layers.) This spacer layer allows you to joint the edge of the design lamination. The glued up lamination will almost never have straight enough edges to allow it to be glued into the bottom of the platter without jointing first. Jointing it without at least a spacer layer would of course cut into the design.

Figure 3-145. Arrow is pointing to the two dowels. Note they are slightly shorter than the design layers.

Cut two 3/16" dowels slightly shorter than the stack of your design layers. Note that the spacer and trim layers are missing in Figure 3-145. Since these layers have nothing to do with the design, it is not necessary to "pin" them during gluing.

Figure 3-146. Gluing up the design layers with pinning dowels in place.

Using the pins to maintain alignment, glue up your design layers. The spacer and trim layers will be added before clamping.

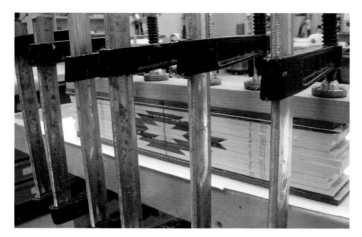

Figure 3-147. Design lamination being glued up. Note the spacer and trim pieces have been added to the lamination.

Always use plenty of clamps and a thick glue block when gluing up a lamination. Also, with this many layers to apply glue to, it is a good idea to have two people applying glue. You will not have unlimited "open" time. It's often easier to clamp your lamination to a flat bench as shown in Figure 3-147.

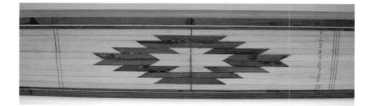

Figure 3-148. Lamination after it has come out of the clamps.

Your lamination should look like the one in Figure 3-148. Before you re-saw it into two pieces, square it up and trim to length.

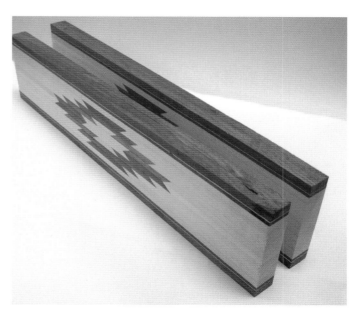

Figure 3-149. Re-sawing and trimming the lamination will result in two primary designs.

Re-saw the 2" thick lamination in the band saw or table saw. Run it through the planer or drum sander to clean up the machine marks left from the saw. The result should be two primary designs, one of which will be glued into the bottom of your platter. The other will go into your next platter.

Spacer 17"
1" 2"
1" 2"
Spacer 17"

Figure 3-150. Drawing of the secondary design for the platter.

3-7: Making the Secondary Design

Making the secondary design for the bottom of the platter is similar to making the primary design. It also will be a lamination made from 2" wide strips of wood. You may chose a design from Appendix B or design your own. For the purposes of this book, I will give instruction for making a chain design as shown in Figure 3-150. The design layers require pieces of wood with contrasting colors in 1" and 2" lengths. I will be using Eastern Maple and Padauk. As we did for the primary design, we will make the secondary design 17" long. This allows us to "pin" the lamination.

Let's list the pieces required for this design by layer starting at the top. There will be eleven layers total. Layers one through four and eight through eleven are trim and spacer pieces. The layers five through seven contain the basic chain design. Of course you are welcome to use a different secondary design.

Layer 1—one at 1/4" by 2" by 17" Padauk (trim)

Layer 2—one at 1/4" by 2" by 17" Eastern Maple (spacer)

Layer 3—one at 1/8" by 2" by 17" Padauk (trim)

Layer 4—one at 1/4" by 2" by 17" Eastern Maple (spacer)

Layer 5—six at 1/4" by 2" by 2" Padauk, five at 1/4" by 2" by 1" Eastern Maple (design)

Layer 6—five at 1/4" by 2" by 2" Padauk, two at 1/4" by 2" by 1" Padauk, six at 1/4" by 2" by 1" Eastern Maple (design)

Layer 7—six at 1/4" by 2" by 2" Padauk, five at 1/4" by 2" by 1" Eastern Maple (design)

Layer 8—one at 1/4" by 2" by 17" Eastern Maple (spacer)

Layer 9—one at 1/8" by 2" by 17" Padauk (trim)

Layer 10—one at 1/4" by 2" by 17" Eastern Maple (spacer)

Layer 11—one at 1/4" by 2" by 17" Padauk (trim)

Let's make a cutting list by species of wood.

	THICKNESS	WIDTH	LENGTH	
Padauk:				
Two at	1/4"	2"	17"	trim
Two at	1/8"	2"	17"	trim
Seventeen at	1/4"	2"	2"	design
Two at	1/4"	2"	2-1/2"	design
Eastern Maple:				
Four at	1/4"	2"	17"	spacers
Sixteen at	1/4"	2"	1"	design

Figure 3-151. Secondary design pieces glued together.

Cut the required number of pieces of each species of wood from your cutting list. Each end of each piece should be cut at a 90 degree angle with a good crosscut blade. Friction glue them together following the pattern in your design drawing.

Figure 3-152. Design lamination glued up and out of the clamps.

After the glue is cured, run each of your design pieces through the thickness drum sander to smooth their surfaces. Carefully line up the design, clamp it together and mark reference lines. Drill holes in their ends to accommodate the wood dowels for "pinning." Apply glue and clamp your design lamination together.

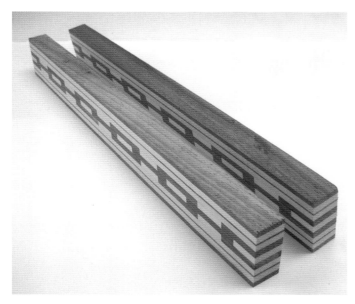

Figure 3-153. After squaring, trimming, and re-sawing, the two secondary designs are now complete.

Square up the lamination and re-saw it into two pieces of equal thickness. Run them through the thickness planer or sander to clean up the machine marks left from re-sawing. You should end up with two secondary design laminations approximately 7/8" thick.

3-8:
Turning the Platter

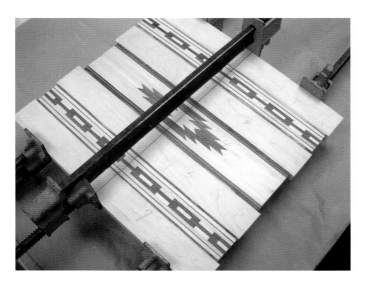

Figure 3-154. Bottom of platter being glued up. Note the center reference line to guide you during gluing.

With both the primary and secondary designs completed, machine out spacer pieces to be glued in between. You'll most likely need to joint the edges of the design laminations for a perfect glue joint. Find the center of your design laminations and draw a reference line across all of the pieces that make up the bottom. I usually number them as well. Apply glue and clamp carefully to make sure all three designs stay on center. Note that no glue blocks are used in this clamping process. It is not necessary because the edges will be cut away and turned into a perfect circle.

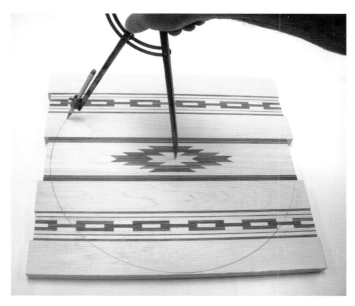

Figure 3-155. Drawing the circle on the glued up bottom.

After the glue is cured, machine the bottom flat in the planer or thickness sander. The bottom should now be approximately 3/4" thick. Not to worry, I have had to plane bottoms down to as thin as 5/8" thick and they still worked fine.

Find the center of the primary design. **(Pay Attention!)** Your platter will look odd if the designs appear to be off center. Make sure you're accurate when finding the center. Place a compass point on the center and draw a circle about 1/2" larger than the inside dimension of the rabbet joint that you turned into the segmented ring. Cut the bottom into a circle following this line.

Prepare a plywood faceplate about 7" in diameter and cut some card stock to fit. **(Pay Attention!)** For smaller diameter platters you will use a smaller diameter faceplate. The plywood faceplate should be about an inch less than half the diameter of your platter.

Figure 3-156. Drawing the circle for the plywood faceplate.

Using the same center, draw a circle slightly larger than the plywood faceplate. Apply glue inside the circle and to one side of the plywood faceplate. With the paper in between, carefully clamp the faceplate inside the circle. Although segmented platters are very easy to turn, I recommend **mini lathe** users continue to double the thickness of their plywood faceplates.

Figure 3-157. Sanding to the exact diameter.

Attach the metal faceplate to the plywood faceplate and mount the bottom on the lathe. Turn it into a perfect circle that will "slip fit" into the rabbet joint that you turned into the segmented ring. Turn the final diameter **slowly.** With your segmented ring, check the fit often as you approach the exact size. I recommend you sand

to the final diameter. A sloppy fit here is not acceptable. Everyone that picks up your platter will turn it over and look at the bottom.

Figure 3-158. Turning a "dish" into the bottom of the platter.

You must turn a "dish" into the bottom prior to attaching the segmented ring. Measure the thickness of the bottom before you start turning the "dish." It should be about 5/8" to 3/4" thick at this point. This measurement will indicate how much you will turn away when making the "dish." For example, if the bottom is 3/4" thick, you will turn away 3/8" at the center and taper the "dish" to a 3/4" wide "flat" on the outer edge.

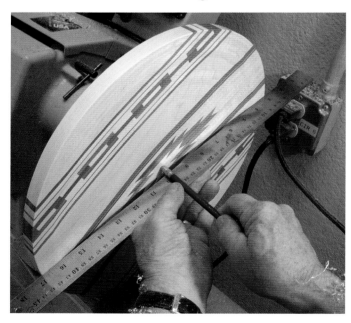

Figure 3-159. Checking the amount of "dish" in the bottom.

Check the depth of the "dish" with a straight edge. The bottom should be about 3/8" thick in the center when finished. Make sure you leave a "flat" of about 3/4" wide around the perimeter of the bottom. This "flat" will be glued into the rabbet you turned on the segmented ring.

Figure 3-160. Sanding the bottom of the platter.

When you have completed turning the "dish," sand the bottom with each grit up through 220. Remember, as with the salad bowl, we intend to never touch the bottom again except with 280 grit abrasive paper.

Figure 3-161. Gluing the bottom to the segmented ring. Note the clamp block on the bottom of the segmented ring.

With the "dish" completed and the bottom turned for a "slip" fit into the segmented ring, carefully apply glue and clamp the two together. Remember, you always apply glue to both surfaces, but apply small amounts. You do not want any glue to squeeze out. Use a clamp block next to the segmented ring. It is not necessary to clamp block the bottom (on top in Figure 3-161), as you'll turn this portion away to form the platter's final shape.

Figure 3-162. Platter mounted on the lathe ready to be turned to its final shape.

After the glue has cured, re-mount the platter on the lathe. Obviously, you must turn off the paper left over from the glue joint and finish turning the platter to its shape.

Figure 3-163. Turning away the left over paper from the glue joint.

After turning off the left over paper, proceed to turn the platter to its final shape. Start by turning the lip and the inside of the segmented ring. Remember, like the bowls, we intend to never touch the bottom of the platter with the lathe tool. The thickness of the lip should be about 1/4" or thinner when finished.

Figure 3-164. The bottom of the platter has not yet been turned.

After completing the lip and the inside of the segmented rings, we must turn our attention to the bottom of the platter. As you can see in Figure 3-164, the bottom is still full thickness on the back side.

Figure 3-165. Turning the bottom of the platter.

Reposition the tool rest to the back side of your platter. Start about two inches from the plywood faceplate and begin turning the bottom of the platter to a pleasing shape. You are trying to taper the bottom of the platter from approximately 3/8" thick at the start of your cut to 1/4"

thick where the bottom joins the segmented ring. The flat portion of the platter (the base that it sits on) should be slightly more than half the diameter of the entire platter.

Figure 3-166. Completed platter ready for final sanding.

With the bottom of the platter turned to its final shape, sand the bottom, the lip, and the inside of the segmented ring. Remember not to sand the face of the bottom of the platter until you reach 280 grit abrasive paper.

Figure 3-167. Removing the plywood faceplate.

Remove the plywood faceplate with a chisel and mallet as before with the salad bowl.

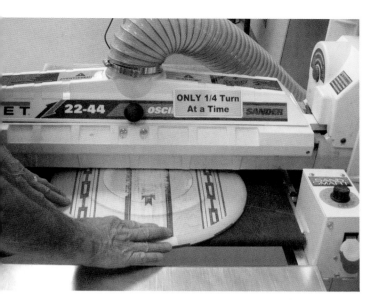

Figure 3-168. Removing the paper from the glue joint in the drum sander.

The platter will be thin enough to remove the paper and glue from the bottom using the drum thickness sander. Be sure to feed the platter "with the grain" through the sander. It's no fun to sand out cross grain scratches.

Figure 3-169. Finish sanding the bottom of the platter.

Finish sanding the bottom up through 280 grit abrasive paper. I recommend using Salad Bowl Finish™ on the platter as most people will use it to serve food.

Figure 3-170. Completed 15-1/2" platter.

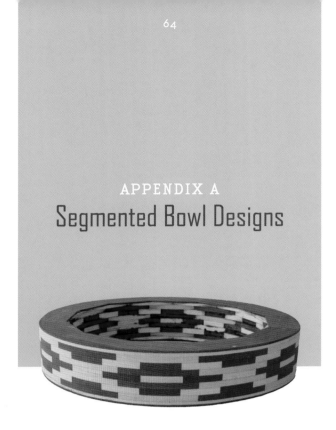

APPENDIX A
Segmented Bowl Designs

The following pages contain several photos of glued up design rings and the number of segments required to make each design. This is by no means all of the designs available to you when making segmented bowls. The number of designs is only limited by your imagination. When making up new designs, I would advise that you draw out your design, list the number and type (light or dark) of the segments required, and keep a permanent record. You may want to return to a design you have made at a later date and keeping a record is an immense help down the road.

In each of the following examples I list the type of wood used in the caption, but of course you may choose to use a different wood for the same design. I list the number of rings, the number of segments in each ring, the type of segment (light or dark) and their placement in order within the ring. I always start with the top trim ring and work my way down in order to the bottom trim ring. "Full size" and "half size" refer to the length of the segments for the bowl you are making. For example, in this book

we started out making a 9 inch diameter L-shaped salad bowl. We determined that the required size for a full size segment was 2-5/8" and half size would be 1-5/16". But, as you know, the length of a segment is determined by the diameter of the bowl you are making, so your full size segment must match your bowl size.

In the examples below, when I list a ring as a design ring, I am referring to rings located between the top spacer and trim rings and the bottom spacer and trim rings.

I have made no attempt to list the segment thickness for each of the designs shown below. When I'm making designs, most of the trim and spacer rings are about 1/16" to 1/8" thick after sanding in the thickness drum sander. Design rings are about 1/4" to 3/8" thick after sanding. However, the thickness of any of these rings may vary to suit your own ideas of a pleasing design. As you will see in the photos below, trim, spacer, and design rings vary to suit my mood at the time I'm making the design.

Figure A-1. Made from Eastern Maple and Purple Heart using 108 individual pieces.

Seven rings are required for this design.

12 full size dark segments for the trim ring.
12 full size light segments for the spacer ring.
24 half size: 6 dark segments, 18 light segments, glue up 3 light one dark, 3 light one dark, etc. for the design ring.
12 full size: 6 dark segments, 6 light segments, glue up every other color for the design ring.
24 half size: 18 dark segments, 6 light segments, glue up 3 dark one light, 3 dark one light, etc. for the design ring.
12 full size light segments for the spacer ring.
12 full size dark segments for the trim ring.

Figure A-2. Made from Eastern Maple and Padauk using 96 individual pieces.

Seven rings are required for this design.

12 full size dark segments for the trim ring.
12 full size light segments for the spacer ring.
12 full size: 6 dark segments, 6 light segments, glue up every other color for the design ring.
24 half size: 12 dark segments, 12 light segments, glue up every other color for the design ring.
12 full size: 6 dark segments, 6 light segments, glue up every other color for the design ring.
12 full size light segments for the spacer ring.
12 full size dark segments for the trim ring.

Figure A-3. Made from Eastern Maple and Padauk using 108 individual pieces.

Seven rings are required for this design.

12 full size dark segments for the trim ring.
12 full size light segments for the spacer ring.
24 half size: 12 dark segments, 12 light segments, glue up every other color for the design ring.
12 full size: 6 dark segments, 6 light segments, glue up every other color for the design ring.
24 half size: 12 dark segments, 12 light segments, glue up every other color for the design ring.
12 full size light segments for the spacer ring.
12 full size dark segments for the trim ring.

Figure A-4. Made from Eastern Maple and Padauk using 96 individual pieces.

Seven rings are required for this design.

12 full size dark segments for the trim ring.
12 full size light segments for the spacer ring.
12 full size dark segments for the design ring.
24 half size: 12 dark segments, 12 light segments, glue up every other color for the design ring.
12 full size dark segments for the design ring.
12 full size light segments for the spacer ring.
12 full size dark segments for the trim ring.

Figure A-5. Made from Eastern Maple and Padauk using 120 individual pieces.

Seven rings are required for this design.

12 full size dark segments for the trim ring.
12 full size light segments for the spacer ring.
24 half size: 12 dark segments, 12 light segments, glue up every other color for the design ring.
24 half size: 12 dark segments, 12 light segments, glue up every other color for the design ring.
24 half size: 12 dark segments, 12 light segments, glue up every other color for the design ring.
12 full size light segments for the spacer ring.
12 full size dark segments for the trim ring.

Figure A-6. Made from American Cherry, Eastern Maple, and Purple Heart using 108 individual pieces.

Nine rings are required for this design.

12 full size dark segments for the trim ring.
12 full size light segments for the spacer ring.
12 full size: 6 dark segments, 6 light segments, glue up every other color for the design ring.
12 full size: 6 dark segments, 6 light segments, glue up every other color for the design ring.
12 full size: 6 dark segments, 6 light segments, glue up every other color for the design ring.
12 full size: 6 dark segments, 6 light segments, glue up every other color for the design ring.
12 full size: 6 dark segments, 6 light segments, glue up every other color for the design ring.
12 full size light segments for the spacer ring.
12 full size dark segments for the trim ring.

Figure A-7. Made from Eastern Maple and Padauk using 216 individual pieces.

Thirteen rings are required for this design.

12 full size dark segments for the trim ring.
12 full size light segments for the spacer ring.
12 full size dark segments for the trim ring.
12 full size light segments for the spacer ring.
24 half size: 12 dark segments, 12 light segments, glue up every other color for the design ring.
24 half size: 12 dark segments, 12 light segments, glue up every other color for the design ring.
24 half size: 12 dark segments, 12 light segments, glue up every other color for the design ring.
24 half size: 12 dark segments, 12 light segments, glue up every other color for the design ring.
24 half size: 12 dark segments, 12 light segments, glue up every other color for the design ring.
12 full size light segments for the spacer ring.
12 full size dark segments for the trim ring.
12 full size light segments for the spacer ring.
12 full size dark segments for the trim ring.

Figure A-8. Made from Eastern Maple and Padauk using 168 individual pieces.

Eleven rings are required for this design.

12 full size dark segments for the trim ring.
12 full size light segments for the spacer ring.
12 full size: 6 dark segments, 6 light segments, glue up every other color for the design ring.
24 half size: 12 dark segments, 12 light segments, glue up every other color for the design ring.
12 full size: 6 dark segments, 6 light segments, glue up every other color for the design ring.
24 half size: 12 dark segments, 12 light segments, glue up every other color for the design ring.
12 full size: 6 dark segments, 6 light segments, glue up every other color for the design ring.
24 half size: 12 dark segments, 12 light segments, glue up every other color for the design ring.
12 full size: 6 dark segments, 6 light segments, glue up every other color for the design ring.
12 full size light segments for the spacer ring.
12 full size dark segments for the trim ring.

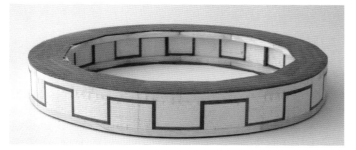

Figure A-9. Made from Eastern Maple and Purple Heart using 120 individual pieces.

Five rings are required for this design.

12 full size dark segments for the trim ring.
12 full size light segments for the spacer ring.
(Pay attention!) 24 half size light segments (cut short to accommodate vertical piece): 12 with the dark strip on top and 12 with the dark strip on the bottom and a vertical dark strip glued in between to make the design in the ring. A full explanation on how to cut and glue this design can be found in Chapter 2-2 starting on page 40.
12 full size light segments for the spacer ring.
12 full size dark segments for the trim ring.

Figure A-10. Made from Eastern Maple and Padauk using 144 individual pieces.

Eight rings are required for this design.

(Pay Attention!) This design requires very careful alignment of each ring for it to be symmetrical. Therefore, I recommend that the end pieces of each half ring be cut about 1/16" longer than the regular half size pieces. This allows the sanding of the half rings without distorting the symmetry of the design. (See the discussion on sanding the half rings on page 20.) Not including the top and bottom spacer and trim rings, this design requires 54 half size light colored segments, 10 of which should be cut long. This design also requires 42 half size dark colored segments, 6 of which should be cut long.

This design is not all that complicated, but it is very easy to get confused during the gluing process. In the list below be sure to glue up the design rings in the order listed. The forward slash (/) indicates the end of one half ring and the start of the next.

12 full size dark segments for the trim ring.
12 full size light segments for the spacer ring.
24 half size segments: 2 light, 3 dark, 5 light, 2 dark / 1 dark, 5 light, 3 dark, 3 light to make the first design ring.
24 half size segments: 1 light, 2 dark, 1 light, 2 dark, 3 light, 2 dark, 1 light / 2 dark, 3 light, 2 dark, 1 light, 2 dark, 2 light to make the second design ring.
24 half size segments: 2 dark, 3 light, 2 dark, 1 light, 2 dark, 2 light / 1 light, 2 dark, 1 light, 2 dark, 3 light, 2 dark, 1 light to make the third design ring.
24 half size segments: 1 dark, 5 light, 3 dark, 3 light / 2 light, 3 dark, 5 light, 2 dark to make the fourth design ring.
12 full size light segments for the spacer ring.
12 full size dark segments for the trim ring.

Figure A-11. Made from Eastern Maple and Padauk using 96 individual pieces.

Seven rings are required for this design.

12 full size dark segments for the trim ring.

12 full size light segments for the spacer ring.

12 full size: 6 dark segments, 6 light segments, glue up every other color for the design ring.

24 half size: 6 light segments, 18 dark segments, glue up three dark, one light, three dark, one light, etc. for the design ring.

12 full size: 6 dark segments, 6 light segments, glue up every other color for the design ring.

12 full size light segments for the spacer ring.

12 full size dark segments for the trim ring.

Figure A-12. Made from Eastern Maple and Padauk using 240 individual pieces.

Thirteen rings are required for this design.

(Pay Attention!) This design requires very careful alignment of each ring for it to be symmetrical. Therefore, I recommend that the end pieces of each half ring be cut about 1/16" longer than the regular half size pieces. This allows the sanding of the half rings without distorting the symmetry of the design. (See the discussion on sanding the half rings on page 20.) Not including the top and bottom spacer and trim rings, this design requires 116 half size light colored segments, 24 of which should be cut long. This design also requires 52 half size dark colored segments, 4 of which should be cut long. The design rings, second from the top and bottom of this design, require 16 full size light colored segments, 8 of them cut long. These two design rings also require 8 full size dark colored segments, none of them cut long.

This design is not all that complicated, but it is very easy to get confused during the gluing process. In the list below be sure to glue up the design rings in the order listed. The forward slash (/) indicates the end of one half ring and the start of the next.

12 full size dark segments for the trim ring.

12 full size light segments for the spacer ring.

24 half size segments: 2 light, 1 dark, 5 light, 1 dark, 3 light / 2 light, 1 dark, 5 light, 1 dark, 3 light to make the top design ring.

12 full size segments: 1 light, 1 dark, 2 light, 1 dark, 1 light / 1 light, 1 dark, 2 light, 1dark, 1 light to make the second design ring.

24 half size segments: 1 light, 1 dark, 1 light, 1 dark, 3 light, 1 dark, 1 light, 1 dark, 2 light / 1 light, 1 dark, 1 light, 1 dark, 3 light, 1 dark, 1 light, 1 dark, 2 light to make the third design ring.

24 half size segments: 1 dark, 2 light, 1 dark, 2 light, 1 dark, 2 light, 1 dark, 2 light / 1 dark, 2 light, 1 dark, 2 light, 1 dark, 2 light, 1 dark to make the fourth design ring.

24 half size segments: 1 dark, 3 light, 3 dark, 3 light, 2 dark / 1 dark, 3 light, 3 dark, 3 light, 2 dark to make the fifth design ring.

24 half size segments: 1 dark, 2 light, 1 dark, 2 light, 1 dark, 2 light, 1 dark, 2 light / 1 dark, 2 light, 1 dark, 2 light, 1 dark, 2 light, 1 dark to make the sixth design ring.

24 half size segments: 1 light, 1 dark, 1 light, 1 dark, 3 light, 1 dark, 1 light, 1 dark, 2 light / 1 light, 1 dark, 1 light, 1 dark, 3 light, 1 dark, 1 light, 1 dark, 2 light to make the seventh design ring.

12 full size segments: 1 light, 1 dark, 2 light, 1 dark, 1 light / 1 light, 1 dark, 2 light, 1dark, 1 light to make the eighth design ring.

24 half size segments: 2 light, 1dark, 5 light, 1 dark, 3 light / 2 light, 1 dark, 5 light, 1 dark, 3 light to make the bottom design ring.

12 full size light segments for the spacer ring.

12 full size dark segments for the trim ring.

APPENDIX B
Platter Designs

Designs for platters generally consist of a primary design in the center and a secondary design on either side. There are no hard and fast rules, the designs for platters, like the bowls, are only limited by your imagination and creativity.

The following examples are of primary and secondary designs that I have used in some of my platters. Most of the platters I have made are 12" to 15" in diameter. Adding about 3" for pinning, make the laminations about 14" to 17" long. See Chapter 3-3 (page 50) for a complete discussion of planning a primary design. You'll have to adjust the size of the center design to fit your requirements. Make the designs out of material that is two inches wide so you can re-saw the lamination. Once you re-saw, you'll have two designs from one lamination.

I have also given dimensions for the secondary designs. You may use the dimensions listed for almost any platter you are making. Since, the examples I have given are repeating designs, you'll only have to adjust its total length to fit to the diameter of your platter.

All of the following information for making primary and secondary designs will start with the top layer and work down. No thickness is given for any of the layers in the following examples. Make sure the top and bottom trim layers are thick enough so they can be jointed before gluing them into the bottom of the platter. All layers that have multiple pieces are listed in the order in which they should be glued.

Primary Designs

Figure B-1. Made from Eastern Maple and Padauk using 59 individual pieces.

This design requires 11 layers and can be cut without any special fixtures as all joints are 90 degree butt joints. The following dimensions will result in a 17" long lamination, which allows for pinning. The photo in Figure B-1 has been trimmed down to a 15" length.

Trim layer: 17" in length
Spacer layer: 17" in length
First design layer: 1-1/2" light, 1" dark, 4-1/2" light, 3" dark, 4-1/2" light, 1" dark, 1-1/2" light
Second design layer: 1-3/4" light, 1-1/2" dark, 3" light, 1-1/2" dark, 1-1/2" light, 1-1/2" dark, 3" light, 1-1/2" dark, 1-3/4" light
Third design layer: 2-1/2" light, 1-1/2" dark, 1-1/2" light, 1-1/2" dark, 3" light, 1-1/2" dark, 1-1/2" light, 1-1/2" dark, 2-1/2" light
Fourth design layer: 3-1/4" light, 3" dark, 4-1/2" light, 3" dark, 3-1/4" light
Fifth design layer: 2-1/2" light, 1-1/2" dark, 1-1/2" light, 1-1/2" dark, 3" light, 1-1/2" dark, 1-1/2" light, 1-1/2" dark, 2-1/2" light
Sixth design layer: 1-3/4" light, 1-1/2" dark, 3" light, 1-1/2" dark, 1-1/2" light, 1-1/2" dark, 3" light, 1-1/2" dark, 1-3/4" light
Seventh design layer: 1-1/2" light, 1" dark, 4-1/2" light, 3" dark, 4-1/2" light, 1" dark, 1-1/2" light
Spacer layer: 17" in length
Trim layer: 17" in length

Figure B-2. Made from Eastern Maple, Padauk, and Purple Heart using 40 individual pieces.

This design requires 16 layers and can be cut with the bevel fixture described in Chapter 3-4. The following dimensions will result in a 16" long lamination, which allows for pinning. The photo in Figure B-2 has been trimmed down to a 14" length.

Trim layer: 16" in length
Spacer layer: 16" in length
Trim layer: 16" in length
Spacer layer: 16" in length
First design layer: 7" light, 2-3/4" dark, 7" light
Second design layer: 6-1/2" light, 4" dark, 6-1/2" light
Third design layer: 5-1/2" light, 2-1/2" dark, 1-3/4" light, 2-1/2" dark, 5-1/2" light
Fourth design layer: 4-3/4" light, 2-1/2" dark, 3-1/4" light, 2-1/2" dark, 4-3/4" light
Fifth design layer: 4-3/4" light, 2-1/2" dark, 3-1/4" light, 2-1/2" dark, 4-3/4" light
Sixth design layer: 5-1/2" light, 2-1/2" dark, 1-3/4" light, 2-1/2" dark, 5-1/2" light
Seventh design layer: 6-1/2" light, 4" dark, 6-1/2" light
Eighth design layer: 7" light, 2-3/4" dark, 7" light
Spacer layer: 16" in length
Trim layer: 16" in length
Spacer layer: 16" in length
Trim layer: 16" in length

Figure B-3. Made from Eastern Maple, Padauk, and Black Wenge using 40 individual pieces.

This design requires 16 layers and can be cut with the bevel fixture described in Chapter 3-4. The following dimensions will result in a 16" long lamination, which allows for pinning. The photo in Figure B-3 has been trimmed down to a 14" length.

Trim layer: 16" in length
Spacer layer: 16" in length
Trim layer: 16" in length
Spacer layer: 16" in length

First design layer: 7" light, 2-3/4" dark, 7" light
Second design layer: 6-1/2" light, 4" dark, 6-1/2" light
Third design layer: 5-1/2" light, 2-1/2" dark, 1-3/4" contrasting wood, 2-1/2" dark, 5-1/2" light
Fourth design layer: 4-3/4" light, 2-1/2" dark, 3-1/4" contrasting wood, 2-1/2" dark, 4-3/4" light
Fifth design layer: 4-3/4" light, 2-1/2" dark, 3-1/4" contrasting wood, 2-1/2" dark, 4-3/4" light
Sixth design layer: 5-1/2" light, 2-1/2" dark, 1-3/4" contrasting wood, 2-1/2" dark, 5-1/2" light
Seventh design layer: 6-1/2" light, 4" dark, 6-1/2" light
Eighth design layer: 7" light, 2-3/4" dark, 7" light
Spacer layer: 16" in length
Trim layer: 16" in length
Spacer layer: 16" in length
Trim layer: 16" in length

Figure B-4. Made from Eastern Maple, Padauk, and Walnut using 20 individual pieces.

This design requires 8 layers and can be cut with the bevel fixture described in Chapter 3-4. The following dimensions will result in a 14" long lamination, which allows for pinning. The photo in Figure B-4 has been trimmed down to a 12" length.

Trim layer: 14" in length
First design layer: 6-1/4" dark, 1-3/4" light, 6-1/4" dark
Second design layer: 5-1/2" dark, 3-1/2" light, 5-1/2" dark
Third design layer: 4-3/4" dark, 5" light, 4-3/4" dark
Fourth design layer: 4-3/4" dark, 5" light, 4-3/4" dark
Fifth design layer: 5-1/2" dark, 3-1/2" light, 5-1/2" dark
Sixth design layer: 6-1/4" dark, 1-3/4" light, 6-1/4" dark
Trim layer: 14" in length

Figure B-5. Made from American Cherry and Padauk using 27 individual pieces.

This design requires 7 layers and can be cut without any special fixtures, as all joints are 90 degree butt joints. The following dimensions will result in a 16" long lamination, which allows for pinning. The photo in Figure B-5 has been trimmed down to a 14" length.

Trim layer: 16" in length
Spacer layer: 16" in length
First design layer: 1-1/2" light, 1" dark, 3" light, 1" dark, 3" light, 1" dark, 3" light, 1" dark, 1-1/2" light
Second design layer: 3" dark, 2" light, 2" dark, 2" light, 2" dark, 2" light, 3" dark
Third design layer: 3-1/2" dark, 1" light, 3" dark, 1" light, 3" dark, 1" light, 3-1/2" dark
Spacer layer: 16" in length
Trim layer: 16" in length

Figure B-6. Made from American Cherry, Eastern Maple, and Purple Heart using 40 individual pieces.

This design requires 9 layers and can be cut without any special fixtures as all joints are 90 degree butt joints. The following dimensions will result in a 17" long lamination, which allows for pinning. The photo in Figure B-6 has been trimmed down to a 15" length.

To make the design layer you must first laminate up a 3/4" by 2" wide by 18" long piece of light wood with a contrasting dark wood 2" wide by 3/16" thick glued on top. You must also prepare a piece of contrasting wood 1/8" thick by 2" wide by 14" long for the vertical pieces that will be glued in between. In Figure B-6, a 3/16" thick piece of Purple Heart was laminated to a 3/4" thick piece of American Cherry. It was then cut into pieces 1-1/4" long and glued up with the vertical pieces glued in between. Each 1-1/4" piece was flipped over to complete the Greek

Key design. Then this design must be run through the thickness drum sander to smooth the 2" wide surface for gluing, to reduce the top and bottom lamination to match the 1/8" thick vertical pieces.

Trim layer: 17" in length
Spacer layer: 17" in length
Trim layer: 17" in length
Spacer layer: 17" in length
Design layer consists of the glued up Greek Key design as described above
Spacer layer: 17" in length
Trim layer: 17" in length
Spacer layer: 17" in length
Trim layer: 17" in length

Figure B-7. Made from Eastern Maple, Purple Heart, and Black Wenge using 40 individual pieces.

Figure B-8. Made from Eastern Maple, Purple Heart, and Black Wenge using 40 individual pieces.

This design requires 9 layers and can be cut on the 7-1/2 degree cutoff table that is described in Chapter 1-3. This is the same cutoff table used to cut the segments for a 24 segment ring. The following dimensions will result in a 17" long lamination, which allows for pinning. The photos in Figures B-7 and B-8 have been trimmed down to a 15" length.

To make the design layer you must first laminate up a 3/4" by 2" wide by 36" long piece of light wood with a contrasting dark wood 2" wide by 3/16" thick glued on top. You must also prepare a piece of contrasting wood 1/8" thick by 2" wide by 28" long for the vertical pieces that will be glued in between. In Figures B-7 and B-8, a 3/16" thick piece of Purple Heart was laminated to a 3/4" thick piece of American Cherry. It was then cut into pieces 1-1/4" long on the 7-1/2 degree cutoff table and glued up with the vertical pieces glued in between. By using a 36" long piece and by simply flipping the laminated design piece over each time you make a cut you will end up with two sets of designs. One set will have the Greek Key design with the vertical pieces slanting away from each other as shown in Figure B-7. The other set will have the vertical pieces slanting toward each other as shown in Figure B-8. Both are a unique twist on the Greek Key design. When these designs are run through the thickness drum sander to smooth the 2" wide surface for gluing, the top and bottom lamination will be reduced down to match the 1/8" thick vertical pieces.

    Trim layer: 17" in length
    Spacer layer: 17" in length
    Trim layer: 17" in length
    Spacer layer: 17" in length
    Design layer consists of the glued up Greek Key design as described above
    Spacer layer: 17" in length
    Trim layer: 17" in length
    Spacer layer: 17" in length
    Trim layer: 17" in length

Figure B-9. Made from Eastern Maple and Purple Heart using 33 individual pieces.

Figure B-10. Made from Eastern Maple and Purple Heart using 37 individual pieces.

This design requires 7 layers and can be cut without any special fixtures as all joints are 90 degree butt joints. The following dimensions will result in a 16" long lamination, which allows for pinning. The photo in Figure B-8 has been trimmed down to a 14" length.

    Trim layer: 16" in length
    Spacer layer: 16" in length
    First design layer: 2-3/4" dark, 1" light, 2" dark, 1" light,
        2" dark, 1" light, 2" dark, 1" light, 2-3/4" dark
    Second design layer: 1-1/4" dark, 1" light, 2" dark,
        1" light, 2" dark, 1" light, 2" dark, 1" light, 2" dark,
        1" light, 1-1/4" dark
    Third design layer: 2-3/4" dark, 1" light, 2" dark, 1" light,
        2" dark, 1" light, 2" dark, 1" light, 2-3/4" dark
    Spacer layer: 16" in length
    Trim layer: 16" in length

This design requires 7 layers and can be cut without any special fixtures as all joints are 90 degree butt joints. The following dimensions will result in a 15" long lamination, which allows for pinning. The photo in Figure B-9 has been trimmed down to a 13" length.

    Trim layer: 15" in length
    Spacer layer: 15" in length
    First design layer: 2" light, 1" dark, 1" light, 1" dark,
        1" light, 1" dark, 1" light, 1" dark, 1" light,
        1" dark, 1" light, 1" dark, 2" light
    Second design layer: 2-1/2" light, 1-3/4" dark,
        2-1/4" light, 1-3/4" dark, 2-1/4" light, 1-3/4" dark,
        2-1/2" light
    Third design layer: 2" light, 1" dark, 1" light, 1" dark,
        1" light, 1" dark, 1" light, 1" dark, 1" light,
        1" dark, 1" light, 1" dark, 2" light
    Spacer layer: 15" in length
    Trim layer: 15" in length

APPENDIX C
Gallery

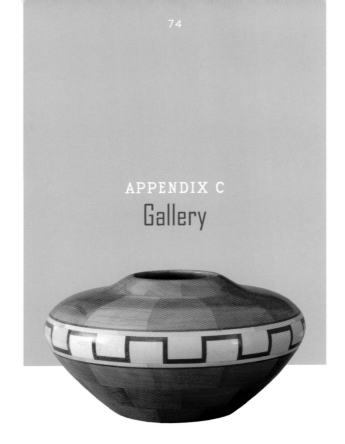

The following pages contain photographs of a small fraction of the segmented bowls and platters I have made. Most of the bowls, either salad or decorator, are about 9" to 10" in diameter. The serving platters vary from 10" to nearly 16" in diameter. I have also included the type of wood and the number of pieces used to make the bowl or platter.

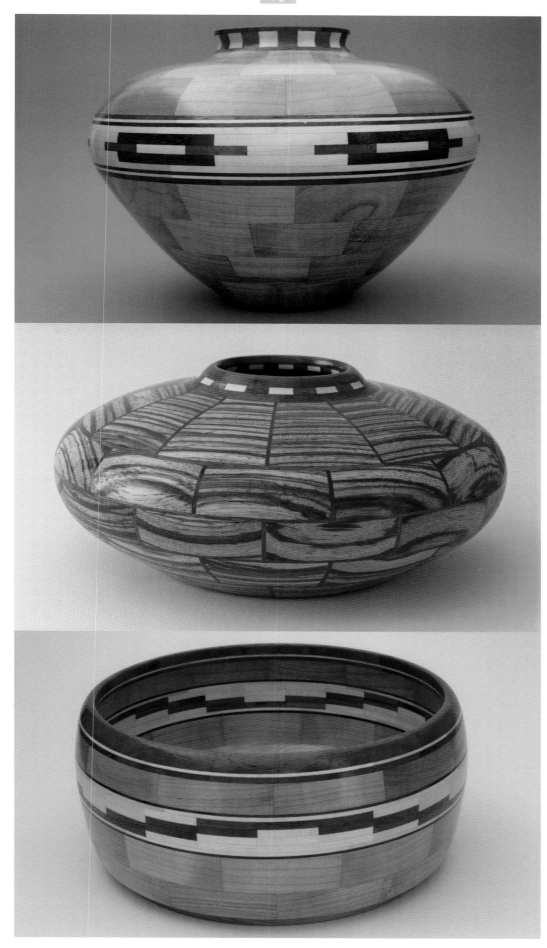

Index